Math Contests
Grades 7 and 8
(and Algebra Course 1)
Volume 3

School Years
1991-92 through 1995-96

Written by

Steven R. Conrad • Daniel Flegler

Published by MATH LEAGUE PRESS
Printed in the United States of America

Cover art by Bob DeRosa

Phil Frank Cartoons Copyright © 1993 by CMS

First Printing, 1996

Copyright © 1996
by Mathematics Leagues Inc.
All Rights Reserved

No part of this publication may be reproduced or trans-
mitted in any form or by any means, electronic or mech-
anical, including photocopy, recording, or any information
storage or retrieval system, or any other means, without
written permission from the publisher. Requests for permission or further information should be addressed to:

Math League Press
P.O. Box 720
Tenafly, NJ 07670-0720

ISBN 0-940805-10-3

Preface

Math Contests—Grades 7 and 8, Volume 3 is the third volume in our series of problem books for grades 7 and 8. The first two volumes contain the contests given in the school years 1979-80 through 1990-91. This volume contains the contests given from 1991-92 through 1995-96, as well as the Algebra Course 1 Contests given from 1993-94 through 1995-96. (You can use the order form on page 136 to order any of our 9 books.)

This book is divided into three sections for ease of use by students and teachers. You'll find the contests in the first section. Each contest consists of 30 or 40 multiple-choice questions that you can do in 30 minutes. On each 3-page contest, the questions on the 1st page are generally straightforward, those on the 2nd page are moderate in difficulty, and those on the 3rd page are more difficult. In the second section of the book, you'll find detailed solutions to all the contest questions. In the third and final section of the book are the letter answers to each contest. In this section, you'll also find rating scales you can use to rate your performance.

Many people prefer to consult the answer section rather than the solution section when first reviewing a contest. We believe that reworking a problem when you know the answer (but *not* the solution) often leads to increased understanding of problem-solving techniques.

Each school year, we sponsor an Annual 7th Grade Mathematics Contest, an Annual 8th Grade Mathematics Contest, and an Annual Algebra Course 1 Mathematics Contest. A student may participate in the contest on grade level or for any higher grade level. For example, students in grade 7 (or below) may participate in the 8th Grade Contest. *Any* student may participate in the Algebra Course 1 Contest. Starting with the 1991-92 school year, students have been permitted to use calculators on any of our contests.

Steven R. Conrad & Daniel Flegler, contest authors

i

Acknowledgments

For her continued patience and understanding, special thanks to Marina Conrad, whose only mathematical skill, an important one, is the ability to count the ways.

For her lifelong support and encouragement, special thanks to Mildred Flegler.

To Mark Motyka, we offer our gratitude for his assistance over the years.

To Brian and Keith Conrad, who did an awesome proofreading job, thanks!

Table Of Contents

The Contests

. . . .

1991-92 through 1995-96

7th Grade Contests

• •

1991-92 through 1995-96

1991-92 Annual 7th Grade Contest

Tuesday, February 4, 1992

Instructions

7

- **Time** You will have only *30 minutes* working time for this contest. You might be *unable* to finish all 40 questions in the time allowed.

- **Scores** Please remember that *this is a contest, not a test*—and there is no "passing" or "failing" score. Few students score as high as 30 points (75% correct). Students with half that, 15 points, *should be commended!*

- **Format and Point Value** This is a multiple-choice contest. Each answer is an A, B, C, or D. Write each answer in the *Answers* column to the right of each question. A correct answer is worth 1 point. Unanswered questions get no credit. You **may** use a calculator.

Copyright © 1992 by Mathematics Leagues Inc.

1. Ten million divided by two million equals A) 5 B) 20 C) 5 million D) 6 million	1.
2. $1.11 - 0.22 =$ A) 0.69 B) 0.79 C) 0.89 D) 1.89	2.
3. The total value of 5 pennies, 8 nickels, and 3 quarters is the same as the value of A) 5 dimes B) 8 dimes C) 12 dimes D) 120 dimes	3.
4. $(10 \times 11) + (12 \times 11) = 11 \times$? A) 11 B) 22 C) 33 D) 120	4.
5. If 2 times a certain number is 12, then 8 times that same number is ? A) 6 B) 24 C) 48 D) 96	5.
6. $\frac{1}{4} + \frac{2}{8} + \frac{3}{12} + \frac{4}{16} =$? A) $\frac{3}{4}$ B) 1 C) $1\frac{1}{4}$ D) $2\frac{1}{2}$	6.
7. Which of the following is *not* a parallelogram? A) hexagon B) rectangle C) rhombus D) square	7.
8. $(360 \times 0.25 \times \frac{1}{9}) \div 10 =$? A) 0 B) 1 C) 9 D) 10	8.
9. The equation $(1 \blacklozenge 1000) + (9 \blacklozenge 100) + (9 \blacklozenge 10) + (2 \blacklozenge 1) = 1992$ is true when each $\blacklozenge$ is replaced by the symbol A) $\times$ B) $+$ C) $-$ D) $\div$	9.
10. One-eighth plus one-fourth equals A) 0.3 B) 0.325 C) 0.375 D) 0.475	10.
11. If you divide my favorite number by any positive number, you will *always* get the same quotient. My favorite number is A) 0 B) 1 C) 10 D) 100	11.
12. 6 hours 54 minutes + 4 hours 56 minutes = ? A) 10 hours 10 minutes B) 10 hours 50 minutes C) 11 hours 10 minutes D) 11 hours 50 minutes	12.
13. Round 1992 to the nearest hundred. A) 1900 B) 1990 C) 1992 D) 2000	13.
14. $1 \text{ km} - 1 \text{ m} =$ A) 90 m B) 99 m C) 990 m D) 999 m	14.
15. $\frac{1}{3} + \frac{1}{6} + \frac{1}{3} + \frac{1}{6} + \frac{1}{3} + \frac{1}{6} =$ A) $\frac{2}{9}$ B) $1\frac{1}{2}$ C) $2\frac{1}{2}$ D) $3\frac{1}{2}$	15.

Go on to the next page ▐▐▶ **7**

16. Which of the following is the measure of an acute angle? A) 89°　　B) 90°　　C) 91°　　D) 100°	16.
17. Which of the following is equal to 14? A) $1 \times 2 + 3 \times 4$　B) $1 + 2 \times 3 \times 4$　C) $1 \times 2 + 3 + 4$　D) $1 + 2 \times 3 + 4$	17.
18. The sum of three *consecutive* integers is 21. The smallest of these three integers is A) 5　　B) 6　　C) 7　　D) 8	18.
19. Which of the following numbers is less than $\frac{7}{8}$? A) $\frac{9}{10}$　　B) $\frac{8}{9}$　　C) $\frac{6}{5}$　　D) $\frac{6}{7}$	19.
20. In triangle *ABC*, $m \angle A = 60°$. Triangle *ABC* will be an equilateral triangle whenever A) $AB = AC$　　　　B) $AB = BA$ C) $m \angle B + m \angle C = 120°$　　D) $m \angle A + m \angle B + m \angle C = 180°$	20.
21. If I have 5 pennies, 5 nickels, 5 dimes, and 5 quarters, the fewest number of these coins I would need to make 47¢ is A) 4　　B) 5　　C) 6　　D) 7	21.
22. If 150% of a certain number is 300, then 100% of the same number is A) 100　　B) 150　　C) 160　　D) 200	22.
23. The reciprocal of a positive number is *always* A) less than 1　B) more than 1　C) odd　　D) positive	23.
24. If *twice* the perimeter of a square is 28, then the length of a side of the square is A) 1.75　　B) 3.5　　C) 7　　D) 14	24.
25. $9 \times 11 =$ A) $10^2 - 1$　　B) 10^2　　C) $10^2 + 1$　　D) 11^2	25.
26. If it takes 6 specks to make a spot, how many specks does it take to make $5\frac{2}{3}$ spots? A) 30　　B) 32　　C) 34　　D) 36	26.
27. 50% of $\frac{1}{50}$ is A) 0.04%　　B) 1%　　C) 10%　　D) 25%	27.
28. Which of the following numbers is closest in value to 1? A) 0.99　　B) 1.1　　C) 1.011　　D) 1.009	28.
29. A rocketship flies at 36 000 km/hr. If I fly 120 km in this rocketship, for how many seconds do I fly? A) $\frac{1}{3}$　　B) 2　　C) 12　　D) 120	29.

Go on to the next page ⦀➡ **7**

7

30. In rhombus *ABCD* (not drawn to scale), *AB* = 10. *Neither* triangle *ABC* nor triangle *ABD* can have a perimeter of A) 40 B) 35 C) 30 D) 25	30.
31. How many positive whole numbers have reciprocals which are greater than 0.001? A) none B) 10 C) 100 D) 999	31.
32. Which of the following inequalities is true? A) $4 \times 5 < 2 \times 10$ B) $4 \times 5 > 2 \times 10$ C) $4 + 5 < 2 \times 10$ D) $4 + 5 > 2 + 10$	32.
33. There are 24 four-digit numbers that can be formed, each using all the digits 1, 2, 3, and 4. The sixth largest such number is A) 3421 B) 3412 C) 4123 D) 4132	33.
34. A 200% price increase is the same as a 50% price increase followed by a _?_ price increase. A) 50% B) 100% C) 150% D) 200%	34.
35. The sum of five unequal whole numbers is 90. The second largest of these five numbers can be *at most* A) 19 B) 41 C) 43 D) 89	35.
36. In a sequence that never ends, each number after the first is half the preceding number. The first four numbers are 16, 8, 4, and 2. Which of the following numbers will *not* occur? A) 0.5 B) 0.125 C) 0.0625 D) 0.005	36.
37. For the year 1992, John will get a $5 allowance on Jan. 1, a $5 allowance on Jan. 6, and a $5 allowance every 5 days thereafter. Under this plan, how much allowance will John get in 1992? A) $73 B) $365 C) $366 D) $370	37.
38. My 12-hour clock runs backwards. If it *now* displays the correct time, then it will *next* display the correct time in _?_ hours. A) 3 B) 6 C) 12 D) 24	38.
39. If the circumference of a circle is numerically equal to the area of the same circle, then a radius of the circle must be A) 2π B) 2 C) 4π D) 4	39.
40. $1 \times \dfrac{2}{3 \times \frac{4}{5 \times 6}} =$ A) 5 B) 1 C) 0.8 D) 0.2	40.

The end of the contest ✍ **7**

Solutions on Page 65 • Answers on Page 122

1992-93 Annual 7th Grade Contest

Tuesday, February 2, 1993

7

Instructions

- **Time** You will have only *30 minutes* working time for this contest. You might be *unable* to finish all 40 questions in the time allowed.

- **Scores** Please remember that *this is a contest, not a test*—and there is no "passing" or "failing" score. Few students score as high as 30 points (75% correct). Students with half that, 15 points, *should be commended!*

- **Format and Point Value** This is a multiple-choice contest. Each answer is an A, B, C, or D. Write each answer in the *Answers* column to the right of each question. A correct answer is worth 1 point. Unanswered questions get no credit. You **may** use a calculator.

Copyright © 1993 by Mathematics Leagues Inc.

1. One-million minus one-thousand is A) 99 900 B) 990 000 C) 999 000 D) 9 990 000		1.
2. It rained all day every other day one week and it did not rain on the other days. Of the following, which *could* be the fractional part of the week that it rained? A) $\frac{1}{2}$ B) $\frac{2}{7}$ C) $\frac{4}{7}$ D) $\frac{6}{7}$		2.
3. $1234 - 345 =$ A) 889 B) 989 C) 999 D) 1111		3.
4. In what month does the 300th day of the year occur? A) August B) September C) October D) November		4.
5. $45455 \times 11 = \underline{?}$ A) 50 005 B) 499 905 C) 499 995 D) 500 005		5.
6. When the cost of a candy bar increased from 25¢ to 29¢, by what percent did the cost increase, based on the original cost? A) 4% B) 16% C) 20% D) 25%		6.
7. $12^2 + 43^2 =$ A) 1993 B) 1983 C) 110 D) 55^2		7.
8. The average of $\frac{4}{5}$ and $\frac{4}{10}$ is A) $\frac{4}{15}$ B) $\frac{4}{7.5}$ C) $\frac{2}{7.5}$ D) $\frac{3}{5}$		8.
9. In a right triangle, the legs have lengths of 8 and 15. What is the perimeter of this triangle? A) 23 B) 40 C) 45 D) 46		9.
10. Find the missing number: $\frac{2}{6} + \frac{2}{6} + \frac{2}{6} + \frac{2}{6} = \frac{?}{24}$ A) 8 B) 32 C) 48 D) 64		10.
11. The complement of an acute angle is *always* ___?___ angle. A) an acute B) a right C) an obtuse D) a straight		11.
12. $99 + 98 + 97 + 96 = 100 + 100 + 100 + 100 - \underline{?}$ A) $1+2+3+4$ B) $1+2+3$ C) $1+1+1+1$ D) 95		12.
13. When $\underline{?}$ is divided by 4, the remainder is 1. A) 97 531 B) 55 555 C) 111 111 D) 54 321		13.
14. $\dfrac{1 - \frac{1}{2}}{1 + \frac{1}{2}} = \underline{?}$ A) $\frac{1}{4}$ B) $\frac{1}{3}$ C) $\frac{1}{2}$ D) $\frac{2}{3}$		14.
15. What is the greatest common factor of 2^5 and 2^6? A) 2^1 B) 2^5 C) 2^6 D) 2^{11}		15.

Go on to the next page ⏩ **7**

16. The sum of three consecutive even integers is 60. What is the sum of the next three consecutive even integers?

   A) 78   B) 72   C) 69   D) 66

16.

17. $\frac{1}{30} + \frac{7}{30} + \frac{11}{30} + \frac{13}{30} + \frac{17}{30} + \frac{19}{30} + \frac{23}{30} + \frac{29}{30} =$

   A) 1   B) $3\frac{14}{15}$ C) $3\frac{29}{30}$ D) 4

17.

18. 10% of 90% is

   A) $\frac{9}{100}$%   B) 9%   C) 100%   D) 900%

18.

19. The largest odd integer less than 1000 with *all* different digits is

   A) 999   B) 987   C) 978   D) 975

19.

20. $9^2 \times \sqrt{9} = \underline{?}$

   A) 27   B) 54   C) 81   D) 243

20.

21. What is the average of seven 77's?

   A) 7   B) 11   C) 77   D) 84

21.

22. A square can be divided into 9 smaller congruent squares, as shown. By drawing different lines, it would be possible to divide this square into _?_ smaller congruent squares.

   A) 70   B) 80   C) 90   D) 100

22.

23. The ratio of 5¢ to 25¢ is the same as the ratio of 20¢ to

   A) $1   B) $1.20   C) $1.25   D) $1.50

23.

24. The product of 3 consecutive whole numbers is 1320. The *largest* of these numbers is

   A) 10   B) 11   C) 12   D) 13

24.

25. $\sqrt{1+2+3+4+5+6+7+8} =$

   A) 9   B) $\sqrt{9}$ C) 36   D) $\sqrt{36}$

25.

26. I live on the planet Zork where, each second, every person flies the same distance as that person's height. If I can fly 100 meters in 20 seconds, my height is _?_ meters.

   A) 1   B) 2   C) 5   D) 20

26.

27. If #(Y) means the number of days in the year Y, what is the value of #(1993) + #(1994) + #(1995) + #(1996)?

   A) 1460   B) 1461   C) #(1997)   D) 7978

27.

28. What is the smallest power of 10 that is divisible by 625?

   A) 10^3 B) 10^4 C) 10^5 D) 10^6

28.

29. $\frac{77}{777} \div 7 =$

   A) 1   B) $\frac{11}{111}$ C) $\frac{77}{111}$ D) $\frac{11}{777}$

29.

Go on to the next page ⠿➡ **7**

30. The average of 4 positive numbers is 8. If all the numbers are less than 10, none of these numbers *could* be

    A) 2   B) 3.5   C) 8   D) 9.9

    30.

31. In the correct addition shown at the right, *A*, *B*, and *C* are different non-zero digits. What is the value of *C*?

    $$\begin{array}{r} BB \\ + BB \\ \hline ABC \end{array}$$

    A) 0   B) 6   C) 8   D) 9

    31.

32. $2 \times 3 \times 4 \times 5 \times 6 \times 7 \times 10 \times 14 = 3 \times 3 \times 5 \times 5 \times 7 \times 7 \times \underline{?}$

    A) 2^3 B) 2^4 C) 2^6 D) 2^8

    32.

33. The lengths of two of the sides of an isosceles triangle are 5 and 16. What is the perimeter of this triangle?

    A) 21   B) 26   C) 37   D) 42

    33.

34. Two different whole numbers between 1 and 100 are multiplied together. The number of digits in their product could *not* be

    A) 5   B) 4   C) 2   D) 1

    34.

35. Of the following, which is largest?

    A) $\frac{1}{\pi}$ B) $\frac{1}{2\pi}$ C) $\frac{1}{\pi^2}$ D) $\frac{1}{1993\pi}$

    35.

36. What is the remainder when 10^{99} is divided by 9?

    A) 0   B) 1   C) 2   D) 3

    36.

37. How many 30's must I add together to get a sum equal to 30^3?

    A) 30   B) 60   C) 90   D) 900

    37.

38. The perimeter of a square is equal to the circumference of a circle. If a diameter of the circle is 8, what is the area of the square?

    A) 16π B) $16\pi^2$ C) 4π D) $4\pi^2$

    38.

39. If the Pros won 30% of their games in the first third of this season, what percent of their remaining games must they win to finish this season having won 50% of *all* their games?

    A) 60   B) 70   C) 75   D) 80

    39.

40. The pattern of the first 7 letters of *contestcontestcontest* . . . continues to the right. The 1st occurrence of a "*t*" is the 4th letter of this pattern. The 1993rd occurrence of a "*t*" is the __?__ letter of this pattern.

    A) 6973rd   B) 6974th   C) 6975th   D) 6976th

    40.

The end of the contest ✍ **7**

Solutions on Page 69 • Answers on Page 123

1993-94 Annual 7th Grade Contest

Tuesday, February 1, 1994

7

Instructions

- **Time** You will have only *30 minutes* working time for this contest. You might be *unable* to finish all 40 questions in the time allowed.

- **Scores** Please remember that *this is a contest, not a test*—and there is no "passing" or "failing" score. Few students score as high as 30 points (75% correct). Students with half that, 15 points, *should be commended!*

- **Format and Point Value** This is a multiple-choice contest. Each answer is an A, B, C, or D. Write each answer in the *Answers* column to the right of each question. A correct answer is worth 1 point. Unanswered questions get no credit. You **may** use a calculator.

Copyright © 1994 by Mathematics Leagues Inc.

1. $33\,333 + 77\,777 = 55\,555 \times$?

   A) 1   B) 2   C) 5   D) 10   1.

2. What is the remainder when $48 + 84 + 48 + 84 + 1 + 1 + 1 + 1$ is divided by 4?

   A) 0   B) 1   C) 2   D) 3   2.

3. $3^2 + 4^2$ has the same value as

   A) 5^2 B) 7^2 C) 12^2 D) $2^2 + 5^2$ 3.

4. What is 0.2345, rounded to the nearest thousandth?

   A) 0.23   B) 0.24   C) 0.234   D) 0.235   4.

5. $1 + (10 \times 0) + (100 \times 0) + (1000 \times 0) =$

   A) 0   B) 1   C) 1111   D) 11 101   5.

6. If the sum of two whole numbers is 20 and their difference is 4, what is their product?

   A) 24   B) 60   C) 80   D) 96   6.

7. $2^3 + 2^2 + 2^1 =$

   A) 12   B) 14   C) 2^6 D) 222   7.

8. If each side of a triangle has a different length, and the lengths of two sides are 7 and 12, the perimeter of this triangle could be

   A) 31   B) 26   C) 25   D) 23   8.

9. $999 + 9999 = 1000 + 10\,000 -$?

   A) 1   B) 2   C) 1101   D) $111 + 1111$ 9.

10. If there were a full moon once every 28 days, then at *most*, how many times could the moon be full in one year?

    A) 12   B) 13   C) 14   D) 15   10.

11. $\frac{1}{2} \times \frac{1}{3} \times \frac{1}{6} =$? $\div 6$

    A) 36   B) 6   C) 1   D) $\frac{1}{6}$ 11.

12. I have an equal number of nickels and quarters, and no other coins. Their total value is $2.10. I have ? coins.

    A) 7   B) 14   C) 21   D) 30   12.

13. Of the following fractions, which does *not* equal $\frac{1}{3}$?

    A) $\frac{11}{30}$ B) $\frac{2}{6}$ C) $\frac{12}{36}$ D) $\frac{3}{9}$ 13.

14. Rounded to the nearest 1%, what percent of the letters in the word "Arnold" are consonants?

    A) 33   B) 66

    C) 67   D) 70   14.

Go on to the next page ▐▶ **7**

14

15. What time is it when it is 3540 seconds before 3:58 P.M.?
    A) 1:59 P.M.   B) 2:57 P.M.   C) 2:59 P.M.   D) 4:57 P.M.

15.

16. $(123 \times 999) - (122 \times 999) =$
    A) 122   B) 123   C) 999   D) 1000

16.

17. Which of the following is a factor of $2^4 \times 3^2$?
    A) 25   B) 27   C) 32   D) 36

17.

18. $0.111 \times 1000 + 0.11 \times 100 + 0.1 \times 10 =$
    A) 321   B) 222   C) 123   D) 1230

18.

19. Of the following numbers, which has the most factors of 2?
    A) 16   B) 88   C) 444   D) 2222

19.

20. Which of the following represents 15 hundredths?
    A) 0.0015   B) 0.015   C) 0.15   D) 1500

20.

21. Which is the reciprocal of $\left(\frac{1}{2} + \frac{1}{3}\right)$?
    A) 5   B) $\frac{5}{2}$ C) $\frac{5}{6}$ D) 1.2

21.

22. Four monkeys are in a barrel. The sum of
    their ages 5 years ago was 80. What is
    the sum of their ages today?

    A) 100   B) 89
    C) 85   D) 84

22.

23. $\left(1 - \frac{1}{2}\right) + \left(\frac{1}{2} - \frac{1}{4}\right) + \left(\frac{1}{4} - \frac{1}{8}\right) + \left(\frac{1}{8} - \frac{1}{16}\right) =$
    A) 0   B) $\frac{1}{32}$ C) $\frac{1}{16}$ D) $\frac{15}{16}$

23.

24. The average of eight numbers is 10. What is the average of
    these eight numbers and 1?
    A) 9   B) 11   C) $\frac{81}{2}$ D) $\frac{11}{2}$

24.

25. $\sqrt{16} + \sqrt{64} = \sqrt{?}$
    A) 144   B) 80   C) 48   D) 12

25.

26. In the figure shown, an equilateral triangle
    with side length 2 has a semicircle drawn on
    one side. What is the perimeter of this figure?
    A) $2\pi + 4$ B) $\pi + 4$ C) $2\pi + 6$ D) $\pi + 6$

26.

27. $1 + 2 + 4 + 8 + 16 + 32 + 64 = 128 - \underline{\ ?\ }$
    A) 0   B) 1   C) 2   D) 3

27.

28. The product of all the prime numbers between 1 and 1994 is
    divided by 10. What is the remainder?
    A) 0   B) 1   C) 2   D) 9

28.

29. $\frac{1+2+3}{4+5+6} \times \frac{8+10+12}{3+2+1} =$
    A) 8   B) 6   C) 2   D) $\frac{36}{21}$

29.

Go on to the next page ▐▐▐➡ **7**

30. 0.1% = A) 10 B) 0.1 C) 0.01 D) 0.001	30.

31. If 1 horse weighs as much as 15 dogs, and 3 dogs weigh as much as 8 cats, then 5 horses weigh as much as _?_ cats.

   A) 40   B) 120   C) 200   D) 600

31.

32. $\sqrt{1 \times 9 \times 9 \times 4} =$

   A) $\sqrt{23}$ B) 18   C) 44.65   D) 1332

32.

33. What is the ones' digit of the smallest whole number larger than 1000 whose digits are all different?

   A) 0   B) 1   C) 3   D) 4

33.

34. $\frac{7}{3}$ is how much more than $\frac{3}{7}$?

   A) $\frac{40}{21}$ B) $\frac{21}{40}$ C) $\frac{49}{9}$ D) $\frac{9}{49}$

34.

35. How many positive integers less than 100 *cannot* be written as the sum of two positive integers (not necessarily different)?

   A) 0   B) 1   C) 2   D) 49

35.

36. The perimeter of rectangle *ABCD* is 14. If all its side lengths are whole numbers, its area could not be _?_

   A) 6   B) 8   C) 10   D) 12

36.

37. In 4 hours, through how many degrees does the hour hand of a circular clock move?

   A) 1440°   B) 120°   C) 90°   D) 48°

37.

38. If $1 + 2 + 3 + \ldots + 50 = 1275$, then $51 + 52 + 53 + \ldots + 100 =$

   A) 1325   B) 2525   C) 3775   D) 63 750

38.

39. A number which is the square of an integer is called a *perfect square*. How many integers greater than 1 million and less than 9 million are perfect squares?

   A) 1999   B) 2000   C) 2001   D) 3000

39.

40. When I turn my calculator upside down, the digits 0, 1, 2, 5, 6, 8, and 9 still appear as digits. For example, when I turn my calculator upside down, 65259 remains the same—that is, it stays 65259. How many whole numbers between 100 and 1000 remain the same when I turn my calculator upside down?

   A) 6×7 B) 6×5 C) $6 \times 5 \times 6$ D) $6 \times 7 \times 6$

40.

The end of the contest 7

Solutions on Page 73 • Answers on Page 124

1994-95 Annual 7th Grade Contest

Tuesday, February 7, 1995

Instructions

7

- **Time** You will have only *30 minutes* working time for this contest. You might be *unable* to finish all 40 questions in the time allowed.

- **Scores** Please remember that *this is a contest, not a test*—and there is no "passing" or "failing" score. Few students score as high as 30 points (75% correct). Students with half that, 15 points, *should be commended!*

- **Format and Point Value** This is a multiple-choice contest. Each answer is an A, B, C, or D. Write each answer in the *Answers* column to the right of each question. A correct answer is worth 1 point. Unanswered questions get no credit. You **may** use a calculator.

Copyright © 1995 by Mathematics Leagues Inc.

1. $1995 + 5 + 1995 + 5 + 1995 + 5 + 1995 + 5 = ?$

   A) 1000　　　B) 2000　　　C) 4000　　　D) 8000

   1.

2. Which of the following fractions has a value less than 0.25?

   A) $\frac{1}{5}$　　　B) $\frac{1}{4}$　　　C) $\frac{1}{3}$　　　D) $\frac{2}{7}$

   2.

3. What is the value of $5 \times \left(\frac{1}{3} + \frac{1}{3} + \frac{1}{3}\right)$?

   A) $\frac{5}{3}$　　　B) $\frac{5}{9}$　　　C) 5　　　D) $\frac{5}{27}$

   3.

4. All the figures below consist of the same five squares of equal size. Which figure has the smallest perimeter?

   A)　　　B)　　　C)　　　D)

   4.

5. $2 \div 4 + 4 \div 8 =$

   A) 2　　　B) 1　　　C) 0.5625　　　D) 0.03125

   5.

6. The greatest common divisor of 120 and 336 is

   A) 6　　　B) 12　　　C) 24　　　D) 1680

   6.

7. $11.111 + 1.11 + 0.1 =$

   A) 11.322　　　B) 12.231　　　C) 12.321　　　D) 22.311

   7.

8. What is the correct time 543 minutes after 3:45 PM?

   A) 9:28 PM　B) 12:48 AM　C) 1:28 AM　D) 1:48 AM

   8.

9. What is the sum of all of the whole number factors of 6?

   A) 12　　　B) 11　　　C) 6　　　D) 5

   9.

10. $98\,765 + 12\,345 =$

    A) 11 110　　　B) 11 111　　　C) 100 000　　　D) 111 110

    10.

11. The sum of two different positive prime numbers *could* equal

    A) 2　　　B) 3　　　C) 4　　　D) 5

    11.

12. As shown, a small circle's diameter (with length 2) exactly overlaps a large circle's radius. What is the area of the shaded region between the two circles?

    A) 2π　　　B) 3π　　　C) 5π　　　D) 9π

    12.

13. $33 \times 333 = 11 \times 111 \times \underline{\ ?\ }$

    A) 3　　　B) 6　　　C) 9　　　D) 27

    13.

14. $(13^2 - 12^2) - 3^2 =$

    A) 2^2　　　B) 3^2　　　C) 4^2　　　D) 5^2

    14.

15. One-half of 50% of one-half equals

    A) 0.125　　　B) 0.25　　　C) 0.5　　　D) 12.5

    15.

16. Which of the following is not an integer?

    A) $\sqrt{0}$ B) $\sqrt{36}$ C) $\sqrt{49}$ D) $\sqrt{91}$

    16.

17. If equilateral triangle ABC has side $\overline{BC}$ in common with square $BCDE$, what is the measure of $\angle ACD$?

    A) 270°   B) 150°   C) 140°   D) 120°

    17.

18. Of the following, which is closest in value to 8.01?

    A) 8   B) 8.1   C) 8.11   D) 9.01

    18.

19. Monday, each cookie costs 25¢. Tuesday, they're 6 for $1. For $6, I can buy ? more cookies on Tuesday than on Monday.

    A) 2   B) 12   C) 24   D) 36

    19.

20. $(32 \div 16) + (16 \div 8) + (8 \div 4) + (4 \div 2) =$

    A) 2   B) 8   C) 16   D) 30

    20.

21. The length of a radius of a certain circle is 4. If A and B are two points on this circle, then AB could be equal to

    A) 1   B) 9   C) 10   D) 12

    21.

22. The sum eighty-six hundred plus eighty-six hundredths is

    A) 86 860   B) 17 200   C) 8600.86   D) 860.086

    22.

23. $\frac{19}{19} + \frac{?}{95} = 1995$

    A) 1994   B) 1995   C) 189 430   D) 189 525

    23.

24. Which has the same value as 50 pennies + 10 nickels + 5 dimes?

    A) 2 quarters   B) 4 quarters   C) 5 quarters   D) 6 quarters

    24.

25. Pat the Cat runs at 5 m/sec and skates at 8 m/sec. How far can Pat the Cat skate in the same time it takes Pat the Cat to run 80m?

    A) 50m   B) 128m   C) 240m   D) 640m

    25.

26. $\frac{2}{3} \times \frac{3}{4} \times \frac{4}{5} \times \frac{5}{4} \times \frac{4}{3} \times \frac{3}{2} =$

    A) 1   B) 3   C) 0.5   D) 0.25

    26.

27. The number 39 is ? % of itself.

    A) 1   B) 39   C) 100   D) 3900

    27.

28. $(1 \times 2 \times 3 \times 4 \times 5 \times 6 \times 7 \times 8 \times 9 \times 10) \div (2 \times 4 \times 6 \times 8 \times 10) =$

    A) 1   B) 105   C) 315   D) 945

    28.

29. Ms. Jones can seat all her students in groups of 3 with none left over; but with groups of 2 there is 1 left over, and with groups of 5 there are 2 left over. Ms. Jones can have ? students.

    A) 12   B) 21   C) 27   D) 29

    29.

30. The product of all six whole number factors of 12 is A) 12 B) 36 C) 72 D) 1728	30.
31. If $\frac{1}{4}$ of a number equals $\frac{1}{20}$, then $\frac{5}{4}$ of this same number equals A) $\frac{1}{4}$ B) $\frac{1}{5}$ C) $\frac{1}{16}$ D) $\frac{1}{64}$	31.
32. What year will it be 3700 days from June 30, 1995? A) 2000 B) 2005 C) 2006 D) 2045	32.

33. If a cube has side–length 2, then its volume is _?_% of the
  volume of a cube whose side–length is 4.
  A) 0.125   B) 12.5   C) 25   D) 50
	33.

34. If n is an integer, let $\blacklozenge n \blacklozenge$ be the sum of the squares of n's digits.
  Thus, $\blacklozenge 344 \blacklozenge = 3^2 + 4^2 + 4^2$. The value of $\blacklozenge 345 \blacklozenge$ and _?_ are equal.
  A) $\blacklozenge 12 \blacklozenge$ B) $\blacklozenge 55 \blacklozenge$ C) $\blacklozenge 60 \blacklozenge$ D) $\blacklozenge 444 \blacklozenge$
	34.

35. If, every 2 seconds, a unicycle wheel of ra-
  dius 1m rolls once around without slipping,
  what is the wheel's average ground speed?
  A) 0.5π m/sec   B) π m/sec
  C) 2π m/sec   D) 4π m/sec
	35.

36. $\frac{1}{5 \times 2} + \frac{1}{5 \times 3} = \frac{1}{5 \times ?}$
  A) 6   B) 1
  C) $\frac{5}{6}$ D) $\frac{6}{5}$
	36.

37. If a regular hexagon and a regular octagon have equal perime-
  ters, what is the ratio of their side–lengths, hexagon to octagon?
  A) 1:1   B) 2:1   C) 3:4   D) 4:3
	37.

38. The product of the first 100 prime numbers is *not* divisible by A) 44 B) 55 C) 66 D) 77	38.
39. The least common multiple of 1, 2, 3, 4, 5, 6, 7, 8, 9, and 10 is A) 1 B) 1260 C) 2520 D) 3 628 800	39.

40. For each whole number $n > 1$, list all the fractions *between* 0 and
  1 with denominator n and a whole number numerator. The list,
  which begins $\frac{1}{2}, \frac{1}{3}, \frac{2}{3}, \frac{1}{4}, \frac{2}{4}, \frac{3}{4}, \frac{1}{5}, \ldots$, continues in increas-
  ing order for each denominator. The 1000th such fraction is
  A) $\frac{8}{46}$ B) $\frac{9}{46}$ C) $\frac{10}{46}$ D) $\frac{11}{46}$
	40.

The end of the contest **7**

Solutions on Page 77 • Answers on Page 125

1995-96 Annual 7th Grade Contest

Tuesday, February 6, 1996

7

Instructions

- **Time** You will have only *30 minutes* working time for this contest. You might be *unable* to finish all 40 questions in the time allowed.

- **Scores** Please remember that *this is a contest, not a test*—and there is no "passing" or "failing" score. Few students score as high as 30 points (75% correct). Students with half that, 15 points, *should be commended!*

- **Format and Point Value** This is a multiple-choice contest. Each answer is an A, B, C, or D. Write each answer in the *Answers* column to the right of each question. A correct answer is worth 1 point. Unanswered questions get no credit. You **may** use a calculator.

Copyright © 1996 by Mathematics Leagues Inc.

1. $(1996 - 1996) \times (1996 + 1996) =$ A) 0 B) 1996 C) 3992 D) 1996^2	1.
2. Of the following, which is a multiple of 7? A) 141 427 B) 141 439 C) 141 441 D) 141 456	2.
3. In any year in which January 1st falls on a Sunday, how many Thursdays will there be in March? A) 4 B) 5 C) 6 D) 7	3.
4. Of the following, which number is largest? A) 500 hundredths B) 40 tenths C) 3 D) 2000 thousandths	4.
5. Which is the product of two consecutive whole numbers? A) 100 B) 99 C) 90 D) 80	5.
6. Of the following, which has the smallest remainder? A) $776 \div 7$ B) $665 \div 6$ C) $554 \div 5$ D) $445 \div 4$	6.
7. $(888+888+888+888) - (777+777+777+777) = 111 \times$ _?_ A) 1 B) 4 C) 7 D) 8	7.
8. I gave two dozen pairs of pears to three pairs of bears. If the bears ate equal numbers of pears, then each bear ate _?_ pears. A) 4 B) 6 C) 8 D) 16	8.
9. There are 25% more new windows in my house than old ones. What is the ratio of the number of new windows to the number of old ones? A) 5:4 B) 9:4 C) 1:3 D) 25:1	9.
10. $81 + 90 + 99 = 9 \times$ _?_ A) 20 B) 30 C) 31 D) 32	10.
11. What is $\frac{6}{5}$ of 6? A) 5 B) $\frac{1}{6}$ C) $\frac{12}{5}$ D) $\frac{36}{5}$	11.
12. The hundreds' digit of the product $(3000 + 400 + 50 + 6) \times 7$ is A) 0 B) 1 C) 2 D) 4	12.
13. If each of the 5 squares shown at the right has a perimeter of 8 cm, then the perimeter of the entire figure is _?_ cm. A) 12 B) 24 C) 32 D) 40	13.
14. Of the following, which has the most *different* primes as factors? A) 30 B) 32 C) 143 D) 144	14.

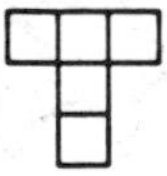

Go on to the next page ⟶ **7**

22

15. Of the following sums, which is the largest? A) $1995+0.1996$ B) $199.5+1.996$ C) $19.95+19.96$ D) $1.995+199.6$	15.
16. $\sqrt{16 \times 25}$ = A) $\sqrt{40}$ B) 10 C) 20 D) 100	16.
17. Write 0.125 as a fraction in lowest terms. Its numerator is A) 1 B) 2 C) 5 D) 8	17.
18. How many of the numbers 0, 0.5, 1, 2 are larger than their squares? A) 0 B) 1 C) 2 D) 3	18.
19. I played video games at the arcade from 10:53 AM to 5:05 PM the same day. At _?_, I was halfway done at the arcade that day. A) 1:54 PM B) 1:58 PM C) 1:59 PM D) 2:04 PM	19.
20. The largest prime factor of 77 000 000 is A) 5 B) 7 C) 11 D) 77	20.
21. At the First National Bank of Inflation, my money doubles every day. If I have \$1 in my account today, it will take at least _?_ more days for my account to have more than \$1000. A) 10 B) 999 C) 1000 D) 1024	21.
22. Writing the result of 1.11111×111.111 requires _?_ digits. A) 8 B) 10 C) 11 D) 12	22.
23. Whether I divide _?_ by 2, by 3, by 5, or by 7, I get a remainder of 1. A) $2 + 3 + 5 + 7 + 1$ B) $2 \times 3 \times 5 \times 7 + 1$ C) $2 \times 3 \times 5 \times 7 \times 1$ D) 23 571	23.
24. If the winning number is $2^3 \times 3^2$, then the winning number is equal to A) 2×6^2 B) 2×6^4 C) 6^5 D) 6^6	24.
25. $\frac{1}{3} + \frac{10}{3} + \frac{100}{3}$ = A) 10 B) 11 C) 33 D) 37	25.
26. $10 \times 20 \times 30 = 1 \times 2 \times 3 \times$ _?_ A) 10 B) 30 C) 100 D) 1000	26.
27. 10% of 100 is what percent of 1000? A) 1% B) 10% C) 100% D) 10 000%	27.
28. If the radius plus the circumference of a certain circle is $6\pi + 3$, how long is the diameter of the circle? A) 3 B) 6 C) 2π D) $6/\pi$	28.

Go on to the next page ⏭ **7**

29. If the sum of the measures of two of the angles in a right triangle is 130°, what is the measure of the triangle's smallest angle? A) 20°　　　B) 30°　　　C) 40°　　　D) 50°	29.
30. A circular ferris wheel's circumference is 72π m. The wheel is supported at its center by a triangular frame 40 m high. How high above ground level is the highest point of the ferris wheel? A) 56 m　　B) 76 m　　C) 112 m　　D) 152 m	30.
31. $\left(2 - \frac{1}{2}\right) \times \left(2 - \frac{2}{3}\right) \times \left(2 - \frac{3}{4}\right) \times \left(2 - \frac{4}{5}\right) \times \left(2 - \frac{5}{6}\right) =$ A) $\frac{1}{6}$　　　　B) $\frac{1}{2}$　　　　C) 2　　　　D) $3\frac{1}{2}$	31.
32. In which of the following pairs are the numbers furthest apart? A) 30^2 & 40^2　　B) 41^2 & 49^2　　C) 62^2 & 68^2　　D) 93^2 & 97^2	32.
33. Which is *not* a factor of the product of the first 100 primes? A) 666　　　　B) 555　　　　C) 222　　　　D) 111	33.
34. Mickey counted to 900 by 2's, beginning with 2. Minnie counted to 900 by 9's, beginning with 9. How many of the numbers that Mickey counted were also counted by Minnie? A) 18　　　　B) 50　　　　C) 92　　　　D) 100	34.
35. If 12 is a factor of the *square* of the whole number N, then it's possible that _?_ is *not* a factor of N. A) 2　　　　B) 3　　　　C) 4　　　　D) 6	35.
36. I have equal numbers of pennies, nickels, dimes, and quarters. The total value of my coins is \$2.05. Altogether, I have _?_ coins. A) 4　　　　B) 5　　　　C) 20　　　　D) 41	36.
37. $(1 \times 1 + 1 \times 2 + \ldots + 1 \times 10) + (10 \times 1 + 10 \times 2 + \ldots + 10 \times 10) + (100 \times 1 + 100 \times 2 + \ldots + 100 \times 10) = 111 \times$ _?_ A) 55　　　　B) 60　　　　C) 63　　　　D) 66	37.
38. Of 200 bears, 150 sing and 60 dance. Of those who dance, 40 sing. How many bears neither sing nor dance? A) 10　　　　B) 20 C) 30　　　　D) 50	38.
39. 1% of 1% = A) 1　B) 1%　C) $\frac{1}{100}$　D) $\frac{1}{100}\%$	39.
40. The hundreds' digit of $1 + 2 + 3 + \ldots + 998 + 999 + 1000$ is A) 0　　　　B) 1　　　　C) 4　　　　D) 5	40.

The end of the contest ☞ **7**

Solutions on Page 81 • Answers on Page 126

24

8th Grade Contests

1991-92 through 1995-96

1991-92 Annual 8th Grade Contest

Tuesday, February 4, 1992

8

Instructions

- **Time** You will have only *30 minutes* working time for this contest. You might be *unable* to finish all 40 questions in the time allowed.

- **Scores** Please remember that *this is a contest, not a test*—and there is no "passing" or "failing" score. Few students score as high as 30 points (75% correct). Students with half that, 15 points, *should be commended!*

- **Format and Point Value** This is a multiple-choice contest. Each answer is an A, B, C, or D. Write each answer in the *Answers* column to the right of each question. A correct answer is worth 1 point. Unanswered questions get no credit. You **may** use a calculator.

Copyright © 1992 by Mathematics Leagues Inc.

1. $1000 + 100 + 10 + 1 = 11 \times \underline{\ ?\ }$
   A) 11   B) 100   C) 101   D) 111

   1.

2. An odd number is divided by 10. The remainder is *always*
   A) 1   B) odd   C) even   D) prime

   2.

3. $1992 - 1000 = 1000 - \underline{\ ?\ }$
   A) –1992   B) –8   C) 8   D) 1992

   3.

4. Each of the following is equal to $111 \times 77 - 770$ *except*
   A) 101×77 B) 100×77 C) 707×11 D) 1111×7

   4.

5. $0.99 + \underline{\ ?\ } > 1$
   A) $\frac{1}{102}$ B) $\frac{1}{101}$ C) $\frac{1}{100}$ D) $\frac{1}{99}$

   5.

6. $50 \times 10 \times 0.1 \times 0.02 =$
   A) 0.1   B) 0.2   C) 1   D) 10

   6.

7. The reciprocal of $(\frac{1}{12} + \frac{1}{16} + \frac{1}{48})$ is
   A) $\frac{76}{3}$ B) $\frac{1}{76}$ C) 6   D) $\frac{1}{6}$

   7.

8. The average of the measures of the two *acute* angles in a right triangle is
   A) 30°   B) 45°   C) 60°   D) 90°

   8.

9. $-1 + 2 + 34 \times 56 + 78 + 9 =$
   A) 1990   B) 1991   C) 1992   D) 1993

   9.

10. The product of a certain number and 7 is 8. One-half of this certain number is
    A) $\frac{7}{16}$ B) $\frac{7}{4}$ C) $\frac{8}{7}$ D) $\frac{4}{7}$

    10.

11. $1000 \div 100 = 100 \div \underline{\ ?\ }$
    A) 1000   B) 100   C) 10   D) 1

    11.

12. If June 1, 2001 is a Friday, then July 1, 2001 is a $\underline{\ ?\ }$
    A) Sunday   B) Saturday   C) Friday   D) Thursday

    12.

13. $0.222 + 0.333 + 0.444 = 1 - \underline{\ ?\ }$
    A) 0.999   B) 0.9   C) 0.1   D) 0.001

    13.

14. The time 1 minute after midnight is
    A) 12:01 A.M.   B) 12:01 P.M.   C) 1 A.M.   D) 1 P.M.

    14.

15. $(20 \times 40 \times 60) \div (2 \times 4 \times 6) =$
    A) 1   B) 10   C) 100   D) 1000

    15.

Go on to the next page ⫸ **8**

16. Which given pair of numbers has the smallest product?

    A) −100,−100   B) −50,−50   C) 75,75   D) 25,25

    16.

17. $1 = \frac{1}{2} + \frac{1}{4} + \frac{1}{8} + \underline{\ ?\ }$

    A) $\frac{1}{8}$ B) $\frac{1}{12}$ C) $\frac{1}{16}$ D) 0

    17.

18. $(10{-}5) \times (10{-}6) \times (10{-}7) \times (10{-}8) \times (10{-}9) \times (10{-}10) =$

    A) 10^5 B) $10^6{-}10^5$ C) 120   D) 0

    18.

19. 5¢ is _?_ % of $5?

    A) 5   B) 1   C) 0.05   D) 0.01

    19.

20. Round (88 ÷ 5) to the nearest whole number.

    A) 16   B) 17   C) 18   D) 20

    20.

21. What is the smallest positive integer that is divisible by 6, by 9, and by 15?

    A) 810   B) 90   C) 30   D) 15

    21.

22. What is $\frac{3}{2}$ of 10% of 10?

    A) 32   B) 15   C) 3.2   D) 1.5

    22.

23. If M is an even integer and N is an odd integer, then _?_ is *always* an even integer.

    A) $M \times N$ B) $M \div N$ C) $M - N$ D) $M + N$

    23.

24. 20% × 30% =

    A) 6%   B) 60%   C) 600%   D) 6000%

    24.

25. A 9-liter pail is filled with water at the rate of ½ liter per minute. How many minutes will it take to fill ⅔ of this pail?

    A) 2   B) 3   C) 6   D) 12

    25.

26. Of the following, which is nearest in value to $9.9^2 - 9^2 - 0.9^2$?

    A) 18   B) 9   C) 8   D) 0

    26.

27. A line is drawn through the center P of rectangle $ABCD$, dividing it into two polygons. If $AB = 5$ and $BC = 2$, these two polygons *cannot* both be

    A) squares   B) rectangles   C) trapezoids   D) triangles

    27.

28. $\frac{2}{3} : \frac{3}{4} = \frac{1}{3} : \underline{\ ?\ }$

    A) $\frac{3}{8}$ B) $\frac{1}{2}$ C) $\frac{8}{9}$ D) $\frac{3}{2}$

    28.

29. If I add 5 of the first 6 positive integers, the sum *cannot* be

    A) 15   B) 18   C) 20   D) 21

    29.

Go on to the next page ⫸ **8**

30. In the diagram, $\overline{OA}$ is a radius of the larger circle and a diameter of the smaller circle. If $OA = 2$, what is the area of the shaded region? A) 2π B) 3π C) 4π D) 7π	30.
31. One million seconds is most nearly equal to A) 1 day B) 12 days C) 1 month D) 12 months	31.
32. How many different integers between 1000 and 10000 each contain all the digits 0, 1, 2, and 3? A) 12 B) 16 C) 18 D) 24	32.
33. *Twin primes* are two prime numbers whose difference is 2. If P is the product of any pair of twin primes, then $P + 1$ is *always* A) odd B) prime C) divisible by 8 D) divisible by 4	33.
34. The product of four consecutive integers is 0. The smallest one of these four integers *cannot* equal A) –3 B) –2 C) 0 D) 1	34.
35. The length of a side of a regular pentagon is an integer. Of the following, which could be the perimeter of this pentagon? A) 1992 B) 1993 C) 1994 D) 1995	35.
36. I am reading a 300-page book in 10 hours, at a constant rate. How many pages have I read in the past 10 minutes? A) 5 B) 10 C) 15 D) 30	36.
37. If $x < 0$ and $xy > 0$, then A) $x < y$ B) $y > 0$ C) $y < 0$ D) $y > 1$	37.
38. When $1^{10} \times 2^{10} \times 5^{10}$ is multiplied out, the resulting number is a __?__ –digit number. A) 10 B) 11 C) 20 D) 30	38.
39. How many of the first 1992 *prime* numbers have reciprocals which are less than 0.05? A) 1972 B) 1984 C) 1985 D) 1988	39.
40. If $\frac{1}{42} = a$, then $\frac{1}{30} = $ __?__ A) $\frac{1}{12}a$ B) $\frac{7}{6}a$ C) $\frac{6}{7}a$ D) $\frac{7}{5}a$	40.

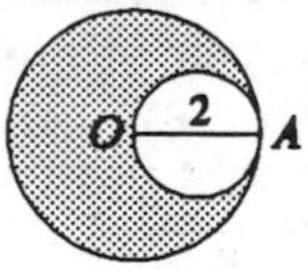

The end of the contest 👈 **8**

Solutions on Page 87 • Answers on Page 127

EIGHTH GRADE MATHEMATICS CONTEST

Math League Press, P.O. Box 720, Tenafly, New Jersey 07670-0720

1992-93 Annual 8th Grade Contest

Tuesday, February 2, 1993

Instructions

- **Time** You will have only *30 minutes* working time for this contest. You might be *unable* to finish all 40 questions in the time allowed.

- **Scores** Please remember that *this is a contest, not a test*—and there is no "passing" or "failing" score. Few students score as high as 30 points (75% correct). Students with half that, 15 points, *should be commended!*

- **Format and Point Value** This is a multiple-choice contest. Each answer is an A, B, C, or D. Write each answer in the *Answers* column to the right of each question. A correct answer is worth 1 point. Unanswered questions get no credit. You **may** use a calculator.

Copyright © 1993 by Mathematics Leagues Inc.

1. Which of the following has a value different from the others? | 1.
   A) 19.92×19.93 B) 1.992×199.3 C) 199.2×1.993 D) 1.992×1.993

2. $63 + 36 + 81 = 61 + 34 + 79 +$ _?_ | 2.
   A) 0   B) 2   C) 6   D) 12

3. Of the following products, which is *smallest*? | 3.
   A) 7×0.7   B) 8×0.8   C) 9×0.9   D) 10×0.1

4. Find the missing number: $2^1 + 2^2 + 2^3 + 2^4 + 2^5 +$ _?_ $= 2^6$ | 4.
   A) 2^3 B) 2^2 C) 2^1 D) 2^0

5. $(10 + 20 + 30 + 40) \div (2 + 4 + 6 + 8) =$ | 5.
   A) 2   B) 5   C) 10   D) 20

6. Of the following numbers, which has the *largest* reciprocal? | 6.
   A) –6   B) –5   C) –4   D) –3

7. Find the missing number: $\frac{3}{6} + \frac{3}{6} = \frac{3}{7} + \frac{?}{7}$ | 7.
   A) 3   B) 4   C) 6   D) 7

8. Which of the following polygons has *no* parallel sides? | 8.
   A) triangle   B) rectangle   C) trapezoid   D) square

9. $\frac{3}{8} \times \frac{5}{6} \times \frac{4}{5} =$ | 9.
   A) 0.2   B) 0.25   C) 0.5   D) 1

10. Find the missing number: $(2 \times 3 \times 4 \times 5 \times 6) \div$ _?_ $= 10$ | 10.
    A) 1×2×3×4×5   B) 2×3×4
    C) 3×4×5   D) 3×4×6

11. The supplement of an obtuse angle is *always* ___?___ angle. | 11.
    A) an acute   B) a right   C) an obtuse   D) a straight

12. $0.09 \times 0.09 =$ _?_ | 12.
    A) 8.1   B) 0.81   C) 0.081   D) 0.0081

13. Sam the Wonder Dog jumped on the table and ate $\frac{4}{5}$ of my pie. What is the percent of my pie *remaining*? | 13.
    A) $\frac{1}{5}\%$ B) $\frac{4}{5}\%$ C) 20%   D) 80%

14. $13^2 - 5^2 =$ | 14.
    A) 8^2 B) 10^2 C) 11^2 D) 12^2

15. What is the least common multiple of 2^5 and 2^6? | 15.
    A) 2^5 B) 2^6 C) 2^{11} D) 2^{30}

16. $(-1) + 101 + (-2) + 102 + (-3) + 103 + (-4) + 104 + (-5) =$ | 16.
    A) 410   B) 400   C) 395   D) 390

Go on to the next page ⫸ **8**

17. If 17% of a certain number is 1.7, then the certain number is A) 1 B) 10 C) 17 D) 100	17.
18. Which of the following is most nearly equal to 2? A) $\frac{19}{10}$ B) $\frac{21}{10}$ C) $\frac{199}{100}$ D) $\frac{1999}{1000}$	18.
19. If the length of each side of square *ABCD* is a whole number, the perimeter of square *ABCD* could *not* be A) 96 B) 152 C) 300 D) 462	19.
20. If $2 \times 6 \times 30 \times 210$ is rewritten as $2^a \times 3^b \times 5^c \times 7^d$, what is the value of $a + b + c + d$? A) 4 B) 9 C) 10 D) 12	20.
21. Which of the following is equal to $\frac{1900}{1992}$? A) $\frac{1900+1}{1992+1}$ B) $\frac{1900+92}{1992+92}$ C) $\frac{1900+92}{1992+184}$ D) $\frac{1900+950}{1992+996}$	21.
22. The average of 10 numbers is 11. The average of these same 10 numbers and 0 is A) 5 B) 5.5 C) 10 D) 11	22.
23. 25% of 16% equals A) 4% B) 9% C) 41% D) 400%	23.
24. The sum of 5 even numbers is *always* divisible by A) 2 B) 3 C) 5 D) 10	24.
25. Jane gets $3.50 allowance weekly. She donates 1/7 of it to charity and spends 1/7 of it on lunches. If she saves the rest, how many weeks will it take her to save $210? A) 60 B) 75 C) 84 D) 100	25.
26. In the diagram, each of the nine small squares has a perimeter of 1. The perimeter of the large square which they form is A) 2.25 B) 3 C) 4.5 D) 9	26.
27. $(88 + 1) \times (88 - 1)$ is 1 less than A) 87^2 B) 88^2 C) 89^2 D) $(88.5)^2$	27.

28. A wheel has a circumference of 1 m. If the wheel rolls 3 km, without slipping, how many complete revolutions does it make?
  A) 3 B) 30
  C) 300 D) 3000
	28.

29. There are <u>?</u> whole numbers bigger than 999 and less than 10 000. A) 9000 B) 9990 C) 9999 D) 10 000	29.

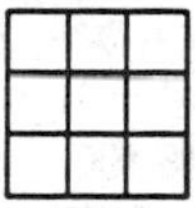

Go on to the next page ⫸ **8**

30. The product of 5 consecutive whole numbers *could* be A) 55440 B) 55444 C) 44444 D) 45454	30.
31. Which of the following is greater than 1? A) $\frac{3}{\pi}$ B) $\frac{8}{\pi^2}$ C) $\frac{\pi}{2}$ D) $\frac{\pi}{\pi^2}$	31.
32. If 6 days ago was Wednesday, what day will it be 701 days from today? A) Tuesday B) Wednesday C) Thursday D) Friday	32.
33. If both angles at D are right angles, what is the perimeter of $\triangle ABC$? A) 33 B) 54 C) 56 D) 61	33.
34. From 9 A.M. today until 9 A.M. tomorrow, how many times will the hands of a standard 12-hour circular clock coincide? A) 2 B) 22 C) 23 D) 24	34.
35. What is the fewest number of Sundays that there can be in any one calendar year? A) 51 B) 52 C) 53 D) 54	35.
36. There are 2 red, 3 blue, and 4 green marbles in a bag. I take one marble at a time out of the bag without looking. What is the least number of marbles I must take out to be sure that I have 3 of the same color? A) 3 B) 5 C) 7 D) 9	36.
37. If a is 50% of b and b is 25% of c, then c is what percent of a? A) 75% B) 100% C) 150% D) 800%	37.
38. If $10 + 20 + 30 + \ldots + 990 + 1000 = 50500$, then what is the value of $(10 - 1) + (20 - 2) + (30 - 3) + \ldots + (990 - 99) + (1000 - 100)$? A) 40400 B) 45000 C) 45450 D) 50000	38.
39. A *perfect cube* is an integer that can be expressed as the product of three equal integers. How many of the first 1 million positive integers are *perfect cubes*? A) 100 B) 1000 C) 10000 D) 333333	39.
40. Each month, Dad gives me $1 on the 1st day, $2 on the 2nd day, $3 on the 3rd day, and, in general, $n on the nth day of the month. During 1992, Dad gave me a total of _?_. A) $5395 B) $5738 C) $5767 D) $5797	40.

The end of the contest ✍ **8**

1993-94 Annual 8th Grade Contest

Tuesday, February 1, 1994

Instructions

- **Time** You will have only *30 minutes* working time for this contest. You might be *unable* to finish all 40 questions in the time allowed.

- **Scores** Please remember that *this is a contest, not a test*—and there is no "passing" or "failing" score. Few students score as high as 30 points (75% correct). Students with half that, 15 points, *should be commended!*

- **Format and Point Value** This is a multiple-choice contest. Each answer is an A, B, C, or D. Write each answer in the *Answers* column to the right of each question. A correct answer is worth 1 point. Unanswered questions get no credit. You **may** use a calculator.

Copyright © 1994 by Mathematics Leagues Inc.

1. $2 + 4 + 8 + 16 + 32 + 64 = (1 + 2 + 4 + 8 + 16 + 32) \times \underline{?}$
   A) 2 B) 12 C) 63 D) 64

2. In value, 5 quarters + 5 pennies = 5 dimes + $\underline{?}$ nickels.
   A) 5 B) 10 C) 16 D) 80

3. $19.94 - 1.993 =$
   A) 0.01 B) 1.01 C) 17.947 D) 18.01

4. What is the sum of all the whole number divisors of 8?
   A) 16 B) 15 C) 8 D) 7

5. If today is Tuesday, what day will it be in 1994 days?
   A) Monday B) Wednesday C) Thursday D) Saturday

6. Of the following, which is largest?
   A) $\frac{1}{1}$ B) $\frac{22}{2}$ C) $\frac{444}{44}$ D) $\frac{8888}{888}$

7. What is the reciprocal of $\left(\frac{1}{9} + \frac{1}{11}\right)$?
   A) 10 B) 20 C) $\frac{99}{2}$ D) $\frac{99}{20}$

8. If the sum of two integers is 0 and their difference is 10, what is their product?
   A) −25 B) 10 C) 5 D) 0

9. The sum of any *two* angles in an equilateral triangle is $\underline{?}$.
   A) 180° B) 120° C) 90° D) 60°

10. $\left(1 - \frac{1}{2}\right) + \left(\frac{1}{2} - \frac{1}{3}\right) + \left(\frac{1}{3} - \frac{1}{4}\right) + \left(\frac{1}{4} - \frac{1}{5}\right) = \underline{?}$
    A) $\frac{1}{5}$ B) $\frac{1}{6}$ C) $\frac{4}{5}$ D) $\frac{5}{6}$

11. $\sqrt{81} + \sqrt{100} + \sqrt{121} = \sqrt{?}$
    A) 5.48 B) 17.38 C) 30 D) 900

12. $10 \times 0.1 + 100 \times 0.09 + 1000 \times 0.009 + 10\,000 \times 0.0004 =$
    A) 1.994 B) 2.3 C) 23 D) 1994

13. Of the following numbers, which has the most factors of 3?
    A) 81 B) 999 C) 2727 D) 3333

14. $(333 \times 111) - (303 \times 111) = \underline{?} \times 333$
    A) 30 B) 10 C) 3 D) 1

15. What is 40% of 40?
    A) 1 B) 16 C) 40 D) 1600

16. What is the remainder when $(125+250+375+500+1+1+1+1+1)$ is divided by 5?
    A) 0 B) 1 C) 2 D) 4

17. $\left(-\frac{5}{5}\right) \times \left(-\frac{4}{4}\right) \times \left(-\frac{3}{3}\right) \times \left(-\frac{2}{2}\right) = \frac{?}{120}$
    A) 120 B) 1 C) −1 D) −120

Go on to the next page ⟫ **8**

18. Pat is exactly 1.598 meters tall. Which of the following measurements is closest to Pat's actual height?

   A) 1.589 m   B) 1.590 m   C) 1.600 m   D) 2.000 m

18.

19. Lee multiplied a number by its square root and got a product of 64. What was Lee's original number?

   A) 4   B) 8

   C) 16   D) 32

19.

20. The number 0.5 is what percent of 50% of 1?

   A) 0.5%   B) 25%   C) 50%   D) 100%

20.

21. If #F means the number of sides of polygon F, which of the following products is largest?

   A) #hexagon × #rhombus   B) #pentagon × #triangle

   C) #square × #trapezoid   D) #parallelogram × #rectangle

21.

22. $4 \times 5 \times \left(\frac{1}{4} + \frac{1}{5}\right) = \underline{\ ?\ }$

   A) 1   B) 2   C) 9   D) 18

22.

23. Robin computed the product $2 \times 2 \times 2 \times 2 \times 3 \times 4 \times 5 \times 5 \times 5 \times 5 \times 7$. What was the left-most digit of Robin's answer?

   A) 8   B) 4   C) 2   D) 1

23.

24. Of the following, which number has the smallest reciprocal?

   A) 1   B) $\frac{1}{2}$ C) −1   D) $-\frac{1}{2}$

24.

25. What time is it 4 hours and 59 minutes before 2:58 P.M.?

   A) 9:57 A.M.   B) 9:59 A.M.   C) 10:01 A.M.   D) 10:57 A.M.

25.

26. A soda machine makes 24 liters of soda. The first 12 liters are made at 4 liters/min. The last 12 liters are made at 2 liters/min. How many minutes did it take to make all 24 liters of soda?

   A) 4   B) 8   C) 9   D) 72

26.

27. Of the following numbers, which one is divisible by the greatest number of *different* primes?

   A) 30   B) 36   C) 96   D) 128

27.

28. Which of the following inequalities is *not* true?

   A) $(-1) \times (-2) > (-1) + (-2)$ B) $(-1) \div (-2) < (-1) - (-2)$

   C) $(-2) \div (-1) > (-1) + (-2)$ D) $(-1) \times (-2) < (-1) - (-2)$

28.

29. The length of a diameter of the circle shown at the right is 8. If $\angle ABC$ is a right angle, what is the perimeter of the shaded region?

   A) $8 + 2\pi$ B) $8 + 4\pi$

   C) $16 + 2\pi$ D) $16 + 4\pi$

29.

Go on to the next page ⫸ **8**

30. If the length of a radius of a certain circle is π, what is its area? | 30.
    A) π B) 2π C) π^2 D) π^3

31. What is the value of $\sqrt{16+\sqrt{81}}$? | 31.
    A) $\sqrt{97}$ B) 5   C) 13   D) $\sqrt{13}$

32. The areas of the two squares shown are 9 and 16. What is the length of the hypotenuse of the right triangle? | 32.
    A) 25   B) 7   C) 6   D) 5

33. If $A \blacklozenge B = (A \times A) - B$, then $(3 \blacklozenge 4) \blacklozenge 5 =$ | 33.
    A) 0   B) 6   C) 20   D) 35

34. Which of the following numbers can be written as the sum of 1994 odd numbers? | 34.
    A) 1995   B) 1996   C) 2001   D) 2095

35. $\dfrac{88}{77 \times 66}$ has the same value as | 35.
    A) $\dfrac{0.88}{7.7 \times 6.6}$ B) $\dfrac{0.88}{0.77 \times 0.66}$ C) $\dfrac{8.8}{7.7 \times 6.6}$ D) $\dfrac{8.8}{0.77 \times 0.66}$

36. One side of a rectangle is twice as long as another side. If all lengths are integers, the rectangle's perimeter could be ? . | 36.
    A) 26   B) 27   C) 36   D) 44

37. $(3989 + 3988 + 3987 + \ldots + 1998 + 1997 + 1996) - (1994 + 1993 + 1992 + \ldots + 3 + 2 + 1) = ?$ | 37.
    A) 1994×1994 B) 1994×1995 C) 1995×1995 D) $1994 + 1995$

38. What is the remainder when the product of all the prime numbers between 1 and 100 is divided by 4? | 38.
    A) 3   B) 2   C) 1   D) 0

39. If $a \times a = 9$, then $a \times a \times a$ could equal | 39.
    A) 18   B) 81   C) 729   D) -27

40. At the Belltower School, 99% of the 100 students are girls, but only 98% of the students in grade 8 are girls. Which of the following could be the number of students in grade 8 who are girls? | 40.

    A) 98
    C) 49   B) 97
                          D) 48

The end of the contest 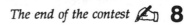 **8**

Solutions on Page 95 • Answers on Page 129

1994-95 Annual 8th Grade Contest

Tuesday, February 7, 1995

Instructions

- **Time** You will have only *30 minutes* working time for this contest. You might be *unable* to finish all 40 questions in the time allowed.

- **Scores** Please remember that *this is a contest, not a test*—and there is no "passing" or "failing" score. Few students score as high as 30 points (75% correct). Students with half that, 15 points, *should be commended!*

- **Format and Point Value** This is a multiple-choice contest. Each answer is an A, B, C, or D. Write each answer in the *Answers* column to the right of each question. A correct answer is worth 1 point. Unanswered questions get no credit. You **may** use a calculator.

Copyright © 1995 by Mathematics Leagues Inc.

Answers

1. $11111 = 10101 + $?
   A) 101   B) 110   C) 1010   D) 110

1.

2. The reciprocal of a negative number is always
   A) negative   B) positive   C) prime   D) 1

2.

3. $3 \times \left(\frac{1}{5} + \frac{1}{5} + \frac{1}{5} + \frac{1}{5} + \frac{1}{5}\right) =$
   A) 0.6   B) 0.12   C) 3   D) 15

3.

4. If a square's side-length is an integer, the square's area cannot be
   A) even   B) odd   C) prime   D) 1

4.

5. $(1995 - 1994) \times (1994 - 1995) =$
   A) –1   B) 1   C) –3990   D) 3990

5.

6. $(1000 \times 0.01) + (100 \times 0.001) + (10 \times 0.0001) =$
   A) 1.0101   B) 10.101   C) 11.1   D) 1.11

6.

7. What month will it be 1000 days after February 14?
   A) October B) November C) December D) January

7.

8. One-half of 1 thousandth =
   A) 0.5   B) 0.05   C) 0.005   D) 0.0005

8.

9. Of the following, which is nearest in value to 0.25?
   A) $\frac{3}{8}$ B) $\frac{5}{16}$ C) $\frac{9}{32}$ D) $\frac{17}{64}$

9.

10. $\dfrac{1}{\frac{1}{2} + \frac{1}{3}} =$ A) $\frac{6}{5}$ B) $\frac{5}{6}$ C) 6   D) 5

10.

11. If the measure of one angle of an isosceles triangle is 20°, then no angle of this triangle can have a degree-measure of
    A) 20°   B) 40°   C) 80°   D) 140°

11.

12. $(10 \div 2) + (20 \div 4) + (40 \div 8) = 60 \div $?
    A) 15   B) 12   C) 5   D) 4

12.

13. Jane has 3 times as many books as Sue and half as many as Bob. If Bob has 12 books, how many books does Sue have?
    A) 2   B) 6
    C) 8   D) 18

13.

14. $(2 + 9)^2 = 2^2 + 9^2 + $?
    A) 0^2 B) 6^2 C) 7^2 D) 11^2

14.

15. $\frac{11 + 22}{22 + 44} = \frac{11}{22} + $?
    A) 0   B) $\frac{22}{44}$ C) $\frac{11}{44}$ D) 1

15.

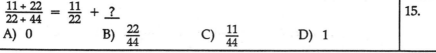
Go on to the next page ⏭ **8**

16. If I first increase five by one hundredth, and next I subtract one thousandth from the resulting sum, then I will get
    A) 4.999　　　B) 4.099　　　C) 5.099　　　D) 5.009

16.

17. $1+1\times1+1\times2\times1+1\times1+1 =$
    A) 6　　　B) 8　　　C) 16　　　D) 32

17.

18. If 40ℓ of maple sap are needed to make 1ℓ of maple syrup, what percent of the original volume of sap is the 1ℓ of maple syrup?
    A) 0.025　　　B) 2.5　　　C) 25　　　D) 39

18.

19. $100\times(70\times50) =$
    A) 7000×5000　　B) 700×5000　　C) 700×500　　D) 7000×500

19.

20. Of 30 students, two-tenths got A's. How many got A's?
    A) 5　　　B) 6　　　C) 10　　　D) 20

20.

21. The value of 25 pennies + 50 nickels + 100 dimes is the same as the value of ? quarters.
    A) 7　　　B) 16
    C) 46　　　D) 51

21.

22. Each side of a triangle has a different positive integer as its length. What is the least possible perimeter of this triangle?
    A) 3　　　B) 6　　　C) 9　　　D) 12

22.

23. 10% is ? % of 50%.
    A) 0.2　　　B) 5　　　C) 10　　　D) 20

23.

24. The product of a positive number and its reciprocal is always
    A) prime　　　B) even　　　C) 0　　　D) 1

24.

25. If $AD = 10$, $\overline{AD} \parallel \overline{BC}$, and the distance from $\overline{AD}$ to $\overline{BC}$ is 4, what is the total area of the 4 shaded triangles?
    A) 5　　　B) 10　　　C) 20　　　D) 40

25.

26. The average of 6 numbers is 7. When a 7th number is added, the average of all 7 numbers is 0. The 7th number is
    A) –42　　　B) –7　　　C) –6　　　D) 0

26.

27. What is the product of $\left(-\frac{1}{7}\right)^{50}$ and 7^{100}?
    A) 50×7　　　B) 7^2　　　C) 50×7^2　　　D) $(-7)^{50}$

27.

28. The number 88 is what fractional part of 888?
    A) $\frac{1}{8}$　　　B) $\frac{1}{11}$
    C) $\frac{11}{111}$　　　D) $\frac{1}{800}$

28.

29. How many positive integers are factors of 30?

    A) 6   B) 7   C) 8   D) 9

    29.

30. $2^4 + 4^2 + 2^4 + 4^2 =$

    A) 8^2 B) 8^{12} C) 12^{12} D) 12^{64}

    30.

31. $17\% = 5\% \times \underline{?}$

    A) $\frac{5}{17}$ B) $\frac{5}{17}\%$ C) $\frac{17}{5}$ D) $\frac{17}{5}\%$

    31.

32. 1 hour and 31 minutes before 2 hours and 59 minutes after 1:41 P.M. is

    A) 3:09 P.M.   B) 3:19 P.M.
    C) 12:12 P.M.   D) 2:09 P.M.

    32.

33. How many integers are their own additive inverses?

    A) none   B) one   C) two   D) three

    33.

34. As shown, a vertex of a square with sides of length 2, and the center of a circle with a radius of 2, coincide. What is the area of the shaded region?

    A) $4\pi - 4$ B) $2\pi + 4$ C) $3\pi - 4$ D) π

    34.

35. If $0.5 < x \le 1$ and $1 < y \le 2$, it is *not* possible that $xy =$

    A) 2   B) 1.5   C) 1   D) 0.5

    35.

36. Of the following, which is closest to $\sqrt{999\,999\,999\,999\,999\,999}$?

    A) 999 999 999   B) 99 999 999   C) 9 999 999   D) 999 999

    36.

37. What is the average of the first 1995 positive integers?

    A) 997.5   B) 998   C) 998.5   D) 999

    37.

38. How far can John's dog go, when it runs at D m/sec, in the same time it takes John to go x m, when he runs at J m/sec?

    A) $\frac{Dx}{J}$ m   B) $\frac{Jx}{D}$ m

    C) $\frac{DJ}{x}$ m   D) $\frac{D}{xJ}$ m

    38.

39. The sum of the squares of the lengths of the three sides of a right triangle is 800. The length of the hypotenuse is

    A) $\sqrt{800}$ B) $\frac{1}{2}\sqrt{800}$ C) 25   D) 20

    39.

40. What is the quotient of the least common multiple of the first 40 positive integers divided by the least common multiple of the first 30 positive integers?

    A) 1147   B) 2294   C) 36 704   D) 89 466

    40.

The end of the contest ✍ **8**

Solutions on Page 99 • Answers on Page 130

1995-96 Annual 8th Grade Contest

Tuesday, February 2, 1996

Instructions

8

- **Time** You will have only *30 minutes* working time for this contest. You might be *unable* to finish all 40 questions in the time allowed.

- **Scores** Please remember that *this is a contest, not a test*—and there is no "passing" or "failing" score. Few students score as high as 30 points (75% correct). Students with half that, 15 points, *should be commended!*

- **Format and Point Value** This is a multiple-choice contest. Each answer is an A, B, C, or D. Write each answer in the *Answers* column to the right of each question. A correct answer is worth 1 point. Unanswered questions get no credit. You **may** use a calculator.

Copyright © 1996 by Mathematics Leagues Inc.

	Answers
1. $(10-9) \times (9-8) \times (8-7) \times \ldots \times (3-2) \times (2-1) =$ A) 1 B) 9 C) 10 D) 11	1.
2. Of the following numbers, which is divisible by 12? A) 102 B) 124 C) 1122 D) 1224	2.
3. $0.5 + 0.05 + 0.005 =$ A) $\frac{111}{200}$ B) $\frac{3}{200}$ C) $\frac{111}{8}$ D) $\frac{3}{8}$	3.
4. Since April 1, 1986 was a Tuesday, March, 1986 had _?_ Mondays. A) 3 B) 4 C) 5 D) 6	4.
5. A jogger who jogs exactly 100 steps per minute will take _?_ minutes to jog 450 steps. A) 4 B) 4.5 C) 5 D) 5.5	5.
6. Which of the following is a whole number? A) $\frac{1996}{6}$ B) $\frac{1996}{9}$ C) $\frac{1996}{12}$ D) $\frac{1996}{1996}$	6.
7. How much greater is 9 hundredths than 8 thousandths? A) 0.082 B) 0.081 C) 0.82 D) 0.092	7.
8. What month will it be 367 days after February 28th? A) January B) February C) March D) April	8.
9. When 0.0709 is rounded to the nearest thousandth, the result is A) 0.0709 B) 0.0701 C) 0.070 D) 0.071	9.
10. What is the sum of the two largest prime factors of 770? A) 14 B) 16 C) 18 D) 21	10.
11. Ali's crystal ball grants two-fifths of one-fifth of all wishes. This is _?_ % of all wishes. A) $\frac{3}{5}$ B) $\frac{2}{25}$ C) 8 D) 60	11.
12. $\frac{1}{3} + \frac{30}{9} + \frac{900}{27} =$ A) 3 B) 37 C) 111 D) 999	12.
13. If the equilateral triangles shown have sides of 2 cm and 3 cm respectively, then the perimeter of the figure is A) 11 cm B) 12 cm C) 13 cm D) 15 cm	13.
14. 100% of 10 is what percent of 1? A) 1% B) 10% C) 100% D) 1000%	14.
15. Write 0.375 as a fraction in lowest terms. Its numerator is A) 1 B) 3 C) 5 D) 8	15.

Go on to the next page ▐▶ **8**

16. My phone rang midway between 10:53 AM one day and 1:05 PM the next day. It rang at
    A) 11:58 PM   B) 11:59 PM
    C) 12:59 AM   D) 1:59 AM

16.

17. How many integers are their own multiplicative inverses?
    A) 0   B) 1   C) 2   D) 3

17.

18. Which of the following expressions is closest in value to 1?
    A) 0.09   B) 1.011   C) $99 \div 100$ D) $100 \div 99$

18.

19. If twice a number is less than the number, the number must be
    A) negative   B) even   C) 0.5   D) a square

19.

20. A rectangle's area is 18 m^2. Its perimeter is 18 m. One side is
    A) 2 m   B) 6 m   C) 9 m   D) 18 m

20.

21. Of the following, which has the most factors of 3?
    A) 81   B) 270   C) 999   D) 3333

21.

22. In a family of cats, there are 2 uncool cats for every 3 cool cats. If these cats have 120 paws altogether, how many cool cats are in the family?
    A) 12   B) 18   C) 30   D) 72

22.

23. $15+30+45+60+75 = (5+10+15+20+25) \times \underline{\ ?\ }$
    A) 3^5 B) 15   C) 5   D) 3

23.

24. $3\,000\,000^2 + 4\,000\,000^2 =$
    A) $5\,000\,000^2$ B) $7\,000\,000^2$ C) $12\,000\,000^2$ D) $25\,000\,000^2$

24.

25. In a right triangle whose area is 12, each leg is as long as the side of a certain square. What is the area of the square?
    A) 12   B) 24   C) 48   D) 144

25.

26. When a certain number is divided by 4, the remainder is 3. If twice that number is divided by 4, what is the remainder?
    A) 0   B) 1   C) 2   D) 3

26.

27. The dimensions of a box are $\sqrt{9}$ by $\sqrt{16}$ by $\sqrt{25}$. Its volume is
    A) 60   B) 3600   C) $\sqrt{50}$ D) $\sqrt{60}$

27.

28. If two pizzas cost as much as three cakes, and if one cake costs $6, how much do five pizzas cost?
    A) $9   B) $30   C) $36   D) $45

28.

29. What is the reciprocal of $\left(\frac{2}{3} + \frac{3}{2}\right)$?
    A) $\frac{13}{6}$ B) $\frac{6}{13}$ C) $\frac{6}{5}$ D) 1

29.

Go on to the next page ⟶ **8**

30. Each side of a triangle is a different length. One side is 6, one side is more than 6, and one side is less than 6. The perimeter of the triangle could *not* be

    A) 13   B) 18   C) 22   D) 24

30.

31. Let $a \blacklozenge b = a + (2 \times b)$. Then $1 \blacklozenge (2 \blacklozenge 3) =$

    A) 9   B) 11   C) 17   D) 36

31.

32. Candy counted to 600 by 6's, beginning with 6. Dandy counted to 600 by 4's, beginning with 4. How many of the numbers that Candy counted were also counted by Dandy?

    A) 50   B) 100   C) 120   D) 250

32.

33. I sold 13 tickets for $29. Adult tickets cost $3 each. Kid tickets cost $2 each. How many kid tickets did I sell?

    A) 3   B) 5   C) 7   D) 10

33.

34. Find the missing number: $\frac{1}{4} = \sqrt{\frac{?}{64}}$

    A) 16   B) 4   C) 2   D) 1

34.

35. Which of the following could *not* be the measures of two of the three angles in the same isosceles triangle?

    A) 40° & 70°   B) 45° & 90°   C) 50° & 100°   D) 60° & 60°

35.

36. The sum of the two prime numbers between 110 and 130 is

    A) 232   B) 240   C) 242   D) 246

36.

37. If a 12-student class averaged 90 on a test, and a 20-student class averaged 80 on the test, then all 32 students averaged

    A) 83.75   B) 84.75   C) 85.00   D) 85.75

37.

38. The square of a certain whole number N is N^2. If 60 is a factor of N^2, it's possible that _?_ is *not* a factor of N^2.

    A) 16   B) 25   C) 36   D) 100

38.

39. I multiplied all ten integers from 1 to 10 by 1. Then I multiplied the same ten integers (from 1 to 10) by 2, 3, 4, 5, 6, 7, 8, 9, and 10 respectively. What is the sum of these 100 products?

    A) 2475   B) 2500   C) 3025   D) 3575

39.

40. In the diagram at the right, each of the 9 small squares has an area of 1. What is the area of the shaded region if its boundary consists of line segments and quarter circles?

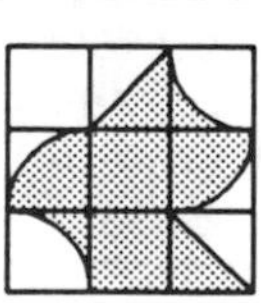

    A) $3 + \pi$ B) $3 + \pi/2$ C) 6   D) 5

40.

The end of the contest ☞ **8**

Solutions on Page 103 • Answers on Page 131

Algebra Course 1 Contests

1991-92 through 1995-96

1993-94 Annual Algebra Course 1 Contest

Spring, 1994

Instructions

- **Time** You will have only *30 minutes* working time for this contest. You might be *unable* to finish all 30 questions in the time allowed.

- **Scores** Please remember that *this is a contest, not a test*—and there is no "passing" or "failing" score. Few students score as high as 24 points (80% correct). Students with half that, 12 points, *deserve commendation!*

- **Format and Point Value** This is a multiple-choice contest. Each answer is an A, B, C, or D. Write each answer in the *Answer Column* to the right of each question. A correct answer is worth 1 point. Unanswered questions get no credit. You **may** use a calculator.

Copyright © 1994 by Mathematics Leagues Inc.

1. If $a = 1, l = 2, g = 3, e = 4, b = 5$, and $r = 6$, what is the value of $a + l + g + e + b + r + a$?

   A) 7　　　　　B) 21　　　　　C) 22　　　　　D) 49

2. If $a = 0$, then, of the following, which has the largest value?

   A) $a + 1$　　　B) $10a - 1$　　　C) $1000a^2 + a$　　D) $1000a^3 + a^2$

3. $(-1)^{100} =$

   A) -1　　　　B) 1　　　　　C) -100　　　　D) 100

4. $(x + 2) + (2x + 4) + (3x + 6) + (4x + 8) =$

   A) $x + 20$　　B) $9x + 20$　　C) $10x + 20$　　D) $20x + 20$

5. $(y + 2)(y - 2) =$

   A) $y^2 - 4$　　B) $y^2 - 2y + 4$　C) $y^2 + 2y + 4$　D) $y^2 + 4$

6. $\dfrac{1 + 2 + 3 + \ldots + 100}{2 + 4 + 6 + \ldots + 200} =$

   A) $\dfrac{1}{200}$　　　B) $\dfrac{1}{100}$　　　C) $\dfrac{1}{2}$　　　D) 100

7. If $y = 1994x + 1994$, what is the value of x when $y = 0$?

   A) -1　　B) 1　　C) -1994　　D) 1994

8. $(x^2)(x^3)(x^4) =$

   A) x^5　　　　B) x^9　　　　C) x^{24}　　　　D) x^{234}

9. $x^2 - 10x + 24 =$

   A) $(x - 12)(x + 2)$　　　　B) $(x - 6)(x - 4)$
   C) $(x + 12)(x - 2)$　　　　D) $(x + 6)(x + 4)$

10. If $x = 10$, what is the value of $x^3 + 9x^2 + 9x + 4$?

    A) 23　　　　B) 194　　　　C) 204　　　　D) 1994

11. Which is the largest of the following numbers?

    A) $2\sqrt{3}$　　　B) $(\sqrt{2})(\sqrt{5})$　　　C) $\sqrt{11}$　　　D) $(\sqrt{3})(\sqrt{3})$

Go on to the next page ⅢⅢ➡ **A**

12. Which of the following equations has *no* integer solution? | 12.

A) $x^2 + 1 = 0$ B) $x^2 - 1 = 0$ C) $x^3 + 1 = 0$ D) $x^3 - 1 = 0$

---

13. There is exactly one pair of numbers (x,y) for which both $x + 2y = 3$ and $4x + 5y = 6$. In this pair, the value of y is | 13.

A) -2 B) -1 C) 1 D) 2

---

14. If $n < 0$ and $p > 0$, which inequality is always true? | 14.

A) $n > p$ B) $-n > p$ C) $\frac{1}{n} > \frac{1}{p}$ D) $\frac{1}{n} < \frac{1}{p}$

---

15. I am thinking of a number. When I subtract 2 from the number, then take 300% of the result, the number I get is my original number. What is my original number? | 15.

A) 0 B) 2 C) 3 D) 6

---

16. If n is an integer, which of the following polynomials is *not* always a perfect square? | 16.

A) $n^2 + 2n + 1$ B) $n^2 - 2n + 1$ C) $n^2 + 4$ D) $9n^2 + 6n + 1$

---

17. $\left(2 + \frac{1}{x}\right) \div \left(x + \frac{1}{2}\right) =$ | 17.

A) $\frac{x}{2}$ B) $\frac{2}{x}$ C) $2x$ D) $\frac{1}{2x}$

---

18. Which of the following polynomials is divisible by $x + 1$? | 18.

A) $x^2 + 1$ B) $x^3 - 1$
C) $x^3 + x^2 + x + 1$ D) $x^3 - x^2 + x - 1$

---

19. $x\Big(x\big(x(x + 1) + 1\big) + 1\Big) + 1 =$ | 19.

A) $4x + 4$ B) $x^4 + 2x^3 + 3x^2 + 2x + 1$
C) $x^4 + 4$ D) $x^4 + x^3 + x^2 + x + 1$

---

20. How many solutions does the equation $|x + 2| = 2x$ have? | 20.

A) 0 B) 1 C) 2 D) 3

---

21. How many *different* numbers satisfy the equation $(x - 2)^2(x - 1)^3(x + 1)^4(x + 2)^5 = 0$? | 21.

A) 4 B) 5 C) 14 D) 120

Go on to the next page ⭢ **A**

22. $\sqrt{\sqrt{32}} =$

    A) 2   B) $\sqrt{2}$ C) $2\sqrt{2}$ D) $2\sqrt{\sqrt{2}}$

23. $(x+1) + (x-2) + (x+3) + (x-4) + \ldots + (x+99) + (x-100) =$

    A) $100x - 1$ B) $100x - 25$ C) $100x - 50$ D) $100x - 100$

24. In a certain circle, the length of a radius is equal to the reciprocal of the length of a diameter. What is the area of this circle?

    A) $\frac{1}{2}\pi$ B) π C) 2π D) $\sqrt{2}\pi$

25. $\dfrac{x^3 + 1}{x + 1} =$

    A) x^2 B) $x^2 + 1$ C) $x^2 - 1$ D) $x^2 - x + 1$

26. $x^{32} - 1 = (x^{16} + 1)(x^8 + 1)(x^4 + 1)(x^2 + 1)(x + 1)(\underline{\ ?\ })$

    A) 1   B) $x + 1$ C) $x - 1$ D) $x^{16} + 1$

27. In the rectangular solid shown, the ratio of the number of square units in the surface area to the number of cubic units in the volume is

    A) $\dfrac{2}{x} + \dfrac{4}{y}$ B) $\dfrac{4}{x} + \dfrac{2}{y}$ C) $\dfrac{2}{x+y}$ D) $x + 2y$

28. Which of the following numbers is *not* a solution of
$(x-1)(x-2)(x-3) + (x-1)(x-2)(x-4) + (x-1)(x-2)(x+10) = 0$?

    A) -1 B) 1   C) 2   D) 3

29. In Professor Tuffguy's mathematics class, 36 students took the final exam. If the average passing grade was 78, the average failing grade was 60, and the class average was 71, how many of these 36 students passed the final?

    A) 14   B) 22   C) 24   D) 29

30. The equation $y = |x + 1| + |x - 1|$ has more than 2 solutions when $y = \underline{\ ?\ }$

    A) 0   B) 1   C) 2   D) 3

The end of the contest ✍ **A**

Solutions on Page 109 • Answers on Page 132

1994-95 Annual Algebra Course 1 Contest

Spring, 1995

Instructions

- **Time** You will have only *30 minutes* working time for this contest. You might be *unable* to finish all 30 questions in the time allowed.

- **Scores** Please remember that *this is a contest, not a test*—and there is no "passing" or "failing" score. Few students score as high as 24 points (80% correct). Students with half that, 12 points, *deserve commendation!*

- **Format and Point Value** This is a multiple-choice contest. Each answer is an A, B, C, or D. Write each answer in the *Answer Column* to the right of each question. A correct answer is worth 1 point. Unanswered questions get no credit. You **may** use a calculator.

Copyright © 1995 by Mathematics Leagues Inc.

1. When $x = 10$, $x(x(x + 9) + 9) + 5 =$

   A) 995   B) 1005   C) 1995   D) 9950

2. $(x + 2)(x + 2)(x - 2)(x - 2) =$

   A) $(x^2 - 4)^2$ B) $(x^2 + 4)^2$ C) $x^4 - 16$ D) $x^4 + 16$

3. $(-1)^1(-1)^9(-1)^9(-1)^5 =$

   A) -24 B) -1 C) 1   D) 24

4. Of the following, which is divisible by $x + 2$?

   A) x^2+4 B) x^3+8 C) x^3-8 D) x^4+16

5. $\frac{1}{10} + \frac{1}{10^2} + \frac{1}{10^3} + \frac{1}{10^4} + \frac{1}{10^5} =$

   A) $\frac{11\,111}{10^5}$ B) $\frac{1}{10^6}$ C) $\frac{111\,111}{10^6}$ D) $\frac{1}{10^{15}}$

6. $(x + 3)(x - 3) + (x + 6)(x + 3) = (x + 3) \times (\underline{?})$

   A) $x + 3$ B) $x + 6$ C) $2x + 3$ D) $2x + 6$

7. How many integers are solutions of the equation $|-x| = -2$?

   A) none   B) 1   C) 2   D) 4

8. The lines $y = 2x + 4$ and $y = -4x - 2$ intersect when $y =$

   A) -1 B) 0   C) 1   D) 2

9. Though Pat's dog runs 2 m/sec slower than Pat, the dog runs three times as fast as Lee. If Lee runs at x m/sec, and Pat races Lee, then, after 10 seconds, Pat will be $\underline{?}$ m ahead of Lee.

   A) $2x + 2$ B) $20x + 20$ C) $30x + 20$ D) 20

10. $x\%$ of $100\% =$

    A) x B) $x\%$ C) $10x$ D) $100x$

11. $(x + 5) - (x + 4) + (x + 3) - (x + 2) + (x + 1) - (x + 0) =$

    A) -3 B) 3   C) $3x + 3$ D) $6x + 3$

12. Of the following, which is largest?

    A) 1995   B) 1^{1995} C) $\left(\frac{1}{1995}\right)^2$ D) $(-1995)^2$

Go on to the next page ⫸ **A**

13. Which of the following is equal to 0 both when $x = 2$ and when $x = 4$, but is equal to 7 when $x = 5$?

A) $\dfrac{5(x-2)(x-4)}{(7-2)(7-4)}$

B) $\dfrac{7(x-2)(x-4)}{(5-2)(5-4)}$

C) $\dfrac{7(x-5)(x-5)}{(2-5)(4-5)}$

D) $\dfrac{4(x-5)(x-7)}{(2-5)(2-7)}$

13.

14. 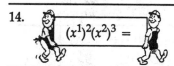 $(x^1)^2(x^2)^3 =$ A) x^8 B) x^{12} C) x^{15} D) x^{18}

14.

15. If n is a positive integer, $n!$ represents the product of the first n positive integers. For example, $4! = 4\times3\times2\times1$. What is the value of $(x-1)(x-2) \times \ldots \times (x-98)(x-99)$ when $x = 50$?

A) $49!$ B) $(2)(49!)$ C) $(49!)^2$ D) 0

15.

16. How many ordered pairs of positive odd integers (x,y) satisfy $x + y = 1995$?

A) none   B) 998   C) 1994   D) 1995

16.

17. What is the area of the region in the xy-plane bounded by the graphs of $x = 1995$, $x = 1996$, $y = 1997$, and $y = 1998$?

A) 1   B) 1995   C) 1996   D) 1997

17.

18. $\dfrac{x+1+\dfrac{1}{x}}{x^2+1+\dfrac{1}{x^2}} =$

A) $\dfrac{1}{x}+1+x$ B) $1+\dfrac{2}{x}$ C) $\dfrac{x^3+x^2+x}{x^4+x^2+1}$ D) $\dfrac{x^2+x+1}{x^4+x^2+1}$

18.

19. Of the following inequalities, which is not *always* true?

A) $|x| + x \geq 0$ B) $-|x| \leq x$ C) $|x| - x \geq 0$ D) $|-x| \leq x$

19.

20. In the alphametic FUN + ON + THE = RUN, each letter stands for a different digit, so that FUN, THE, and RUN are 3-digit numbers and ON is a 2-digit number. If $N = 1, O = 5, U = 7, F = 2$, and $T = 3$, what is the value of R?

A) 4   B) 6   C) 8   D) 9

20.

21. Al and Alice went to a "Bring a Snack" party. Al spent 10 pennies + 16 dimes. Alice spent as much as Al, but her 26 coins consisted of only quarters and nickels. How many nickels did Alice spend?

    A) 16   B) 20   C) 22   D) 24

    21.

22. $\sqrt{x} + \sqrt{x} =$

    A) $\sqrt{2x}$ B) $\sqrt{x^2}$ C) $\sqrt{4x}$ D) $\sqrt{x+2}$

    22.

23. If $x = -1$ satisfies $x^4 - 2x^3 + 3x^2 - 4x + k = 0$, then $k =$

    A) -10 B) 0   C) 2   D) 10

    23.

24. What is the least integer $n > 0$ for which 12^n is divisible by 2^9?

    A) 3   B) 4   C) 5   D) 9

    24.

25. If $x+1995$ represents the smallest of 1995 consecutive odd integers, then _?_ represents the 1995th of these same odd integers.

    A) $x + 3989$ B) $x + 3990$ C) $x + 5983$ D) $x + 5985$

    25.

26. If $xy + 2x + 3y + 4 = 5$, then $y =$

    A) $\dfrac{1 - 2x}{3}$ B) $\dfrac{1 - 2x}{x}$ C) $\dfrac{1 - 2x}{x + 3}$ D) $\dfrac{1 - 3x}{xy + 3}$

    26.

27. Which of the following is divisible by 6 when n is any integer?

    A) $(2n + 3)(3n + 2)$ B) $n(n + 1)(n + 2)$
    C) $(2n + 3)(3n - 2)$ D) $n(n + 2)(3n + 6)$

    27.

28. There is no real number x for which $|x + 1| - |x - 1| =$

    A) 4   B) 1   C) 0   D) -2

    28.

29. For any integer $n \geq 1$, $1 + 2 + 3 + \ldots + (n - 1) + n = \dfrac{n(n + 1)}{2}$. Then, $n + (n + 1) + (n + 2) + \ldots + (2n - 1) + (2n) =$

    A) $\dfrac{2n^2 + n}{2}$ B) $\dfrac{3n^2 - n}{2}$ C) $\dfrac{3n^2 + n}{2}$ D) $\dfrac{3n^2 + 3n}{2}$

    29.

30. Which of the following can be factored into two quadratic polynomials with integral coefficients?

    A) $x^4 + 1$ B) $x^4 + 4$
    C) $x^4 + 9$ D) $x^4 + 16$

    30.

The end of the contest **A**

Solutions on Page 113 • Answers on Page 133

56

1995-96 Annual Algebra Course 1 Contest

Spring, 1996

Instructions

- **Time** You will have only *30 minutes* working time for this contest. You might be *unable* to finish all 30 questions in the time allowed.

- **Scores** Please remember that *this is a contest, not a test*—and there is no "passing" or "failing" score. Few students score as high as 24 points (80% correct). Students with half that, 12 points, *deserve commendation!*

- **Format and Point Value** This is a multiple-choice contest. Each answer is an A, B, C, or D. Write each answer in the *Answer Column* to the right of each question. A correct answer is worth 1 point. Unanswered questions get no credit. You **may** use a calculator.

Copyright © 1996 by Mathematics Leagues Inc.

1. If $M = 1$, $A = 9$, $T = 9$, and $H = 6$, then $\sqrt{M + A + T + H} =$

   A) 5 B) 12.5 C) 25 D) 625

   1.

2. $1 - \left(-\left(-\left(-2\right)\right)\right) =$

   A) –3 B) –1 C) 1 D) 3

   2.

3. If $x^2 = 1$, then $x^4 + 1 =$

   A) 1 B) 2 C) 4 D) 5

   3.

4. $\dfrac{x+2}{x+1} = 1 + \dfrac{?}{x+1}$

   A) 1 B) x C) 2 D) $2x$

   4.

5. Of the following values of x, $\dfrac{1}{x^5 + x^4 + x^3 + x^2 + x + 1}$ is largest if $x =$

   A) 1996 B) 1997 C) 1998 D) 1999

   5.

6. If Terry sold $\sqrt{(\sqrt{100})^2}$ tee shirts, then Terry sold _?_ tee shirts.

   A) 10 B) 25 C) 50 D) 100

   6.

7. If $100a + 100b = 1$, then $\frac{1}{2}a + \frac{1}{2}b =$

   A) 0.5 B) 0.02 C) 0.002 D) 0.005

   7.

8. $(-1)^1 + (-1)^2 + \ldots + (-1)^{98} + (-1)^{99} =$

   A) 0 B) $(-1)^{100}$ C) $(-1)^{101}$ D) $(-1)^{4950}$

   8.

9. If $x = 100$, then $(x - 1)(x - 2)(x - 3) \ldots (x - 99)(x - 100) =$

   A) 100! B) 99! C) 99 D) 0

   9.

10. My cat Boots has $5x$ upper teeth and $3y$ lower teeth. If Boots has the same number of upper and lower teeth, then $x:y =$

    A) 3:5 B) 5:3 C) 8:5 D) 3:8

    10.

11. If $20 \times 40 \times 80 \times 160 = (2^x)(5^y)$, then $x + y =$

    A) 17 B) 18 C) 19 D) 20

    11.

12. The least common multiple of $x^2 - 4$ and $x^2 - 4x + 4$ is

    A) $x - 2$ B) $(x - 2)(x + 2)$
    C) $(x - 2)^2(x + 2)$ D) $(x - 2)^3(x + 2)$

    12.

Go on to the next page ▌▶ **A**

13. If the product of the slopes of two perpendicular lines does *not* equal –1, then the slope of one of the lines must be

A) –1   B) 0   C) 1   D) 10

13.

14. If $x > 0$ and $x^2 - 2x + 1 = 100\,000\,000\,000\,000$, then $x =$

A) 9 999 999   B) 10 000 001   C) 99 999 999   D) 100 000 001

14.

15. If the cost, in dollars, of a box of my favorite breakfast cereal is the same as the number of different values of x which satisfy $(x^2 - 9)^3 = 0$, then a box of this cereal costs

A) $6   B) $3   C) $2   D) $1

15.

16. $\dfrac{1}{x-1} - \dfrac{1}{x+1} = \dfrac{?}{x^2-1}$

A) 0   B) 1   C) 2   D) 2x

16.

17. If (a,b) and (c,d) are the coordinates of different points on the graph of $3x + 4y = 5$, what is the value of $\dfrac{b-d}{a-c}$?

A) $-\dfrac{3}{4}$ B) $\dfrac{3}{4}$ C) $-\dfrac{4}{3}$ D) $\dfrac{4}{3}$

17.

18. How many different values of x do *not* satisfy $\dfrac{2x^2+8x+8}{x^2+4x+4} = 2$?

A) 0   B) 1   C) 2   D) more than 2

18.

19. Wanted: Of the choices below, one is different from the others. Which isn't equal to the others?

A) $\sqrt{16x^{16}}$ B) $4\sqrt{x^{16}}$ C) $4x^4$ D) $4x^8$

19.

20. If $x + 3 = y$, then $x^2 + 6x + 9 =$

A) y^2 B) y^2-6x+9
C) y^2+6x+9 D) $y^2+12x+36$

20.

21. When simplified, the sum of the digits of $(10^{1996} - 1)$ is

A) 1   B) 17 955   C) 17 964   D) 17 973

21.

22. For how many different integer values of x is $\dfrac{2}{x}$ an integer?

A) 1   B) 2   C) 3   D) 4

22.

Go on to the next page ⏩ **A**

23. If $r + \frac{1}{r} = 19 + \frac{1}{19}$, and $s + \frac{1}{s} = 19 + \frac{1}{19}$, and $r > s$, then $rs =$

    A) 0   B) 1   C) 19   D) 19^2

23.

24. Using the "hunt and peck" method, my typing speed, in words per minute, equals the sum of the coefficients of the five terms of $(x+y)^4$. How many words per minute can I type using "hunt and peck"?

    A) 16   B) 12   C) 10   D) 9

24.

25. $\sqrt{7 + 4\sqrt{3}}$ is exactly equal to

    A) $\sqrt{7} + \sqrt{1.18}$ B) $\sqrt{13.9282}$
    C) 3.73205   D) $2 + \sqrt{3}$

25.

26. A circle and a square have equal areas. The ratio of the length of a side of the square to the length of a diameter of the circle is

    A) $\sqrt{\pi}:1$ B) $2\sqrt{\pi}:1$ C) $\sqrt{\pi}:2$ D) $1:\sqrt{\pi}$

26.

27. The graph of _?_ intersects the graph of $y = |x|$ in just one point.

    A) $y = x-2$ B) $y = x-1$ C) $y = x$ D) $y = x+1$

27.

28. Sherlock Hemlock thought of two numbers. Their sum was 20 and the sum of their squares was 300. What was their product?

    A) 15   B) 50   C) 75   D) 100

28.

29. If a and b are the two roots of $x^2 - 5x + 3 = 0$, then $(a+b)(ab) =$

    A) –20   B) 15   C) 20   D) 40

29.

30. In a certain sequence of positive numbers, each term after the second is the product of all the previous terms. If the 1996th term of this sequence is 1996, what is the value of the 1995th term?

    A $\sqrt{1995}$ B) $1996 \div 1995$ C) $1996 \div 2$ D) $\sqrt{1996}$

30.

The end of the contest ✍ **A**

Solutions on Page 117 • Answers on Page 134

Detailed Solutions
•••••••••••••••••
1991-92 through 1995-96

7th Grade Solutions

1991-92 through 1995-96

SEVENTH GRADE MATHEMATICS CONTEST

Math League Press, P.O. Box 720, Tenafly, New Jersey 07670-0720

Information & Solutions

Tuesday, February 4, 1992

7

Contest Information

- **Solutions** Turn the page for detailed contest solutions (written in the question boxes) and letter answers (written in the *Answers* column to the right of each question).

- **Scores** Please remember that *this is a contest, not a test*—and there is no "passing" or "failing" score. Few students score as high as 30 points (75% correct). Students with half that, 15 points, *deserve commendation!*

- **Answers & Rating Scale** Turn to page 122 for the letter answers to each question and the rating scale for this contest.

Copyright © 1992 by Mathematics Leagues Inc.

1. Ten million divided by two million = $10 \div 2 = 5$.
   A) 5   B) 20   C) 5 million   D) 6 million

   1. A

2. $1.11-0.22=1.11-(0.11+0.11)=(1.11-0.11)-0.11=1.00-0.11 = 0.89$.
   A) 0.69   B) 0.79   C) 0.89   D) 1.89

   2. C

3. The total value of 5 pennies, 8 nickels, and 3 quarters equals $(5 + 8 \times 5 + 3 \times 25)¢ = (5 + 40 + 75)¢ = 120¢ = 12$ dimes.
   A) 5 dimes   B) 8 dimes   C) 12 dimes   D) 120 dimes

   3. C

4. $(10 \times 11) + (12 \times 11) = (10 + 12) \times 11 = 22 \times 11 = 11 \times 22$.
   A) 11   B) 22   C) 33   D) 120

   4. B

5. If 2 times a certain number is 12, then 8 times that same number is $4 \times (2 \times \text{the number}) = 4 \times 12 = 48$.
   A) 6   B) 24   C) 48   D) 96

   5. C

6. $\frac{1}{4} + \frac{2}{8} + \frac{3}{12} + \frac{4}{16} = \frac{1}{4} + \frac{1}{4} + \frac{1}{4} + \frac{1}{4} = 1$.
   A) $\frac{3}{4}$ B) 1   C) $1\frac{1}{4}$ D) $2\frac{1}{2}$

   6. B

7. A hexagon has 6 sides, so it is *not* a parallelogram.
   A) hexagon   B) rectangle   C) rhombus   D) square

   7. A

8. $(360 \times 0.25 \times \frac{1}{9}) \div 10 = (360 \times \frac{1}{4} \times \frac{1}{9}) \div 10 = (360 \times \frac{1}{36}) \div 10 = 10 \div 10 = 1$.
   A) 0   B) 1   C) 9   D) 10

   8. B

9. The equation $(1 \times 1000) + (9 \times 100) + (9 \times 10) + (2 \times 1) = 1992$ is true, so the symbol ♦ should be replaced by the symbol ×.
   A) ×   B) +   C) −   D) ÷

   9. A

10. One-eighth + one-fourth = one-eighth + two-eighths = 3/8.
    A) 0.3   B) 0.325   C) 0.375   D) 0.475

    10. C

11. The *only* number which remains the same no matter which positive number divides it is 0.
    A) 0   B) 1   C) 10   D) 100

    11. A

12. 6 hr 54 min + 4 hr 56 min = 10 hr 110 min = 11 hr 50 min.
    A) 10 hours 10 minutes   B) 10 hours 50 minutes
    C) 11 hours 10 minutes   D) 11 hours 50 minutes

    12. D

13. 1992 is between 1900 and 2000; and it is nearer to 2000.
    A) 1900   B) 1990   C) 1992   D) 2000

    13. D

14. 1 km – 1 m = 1000 m – 1 m = 999 m.
    A) 90 m   B) 99 m   C) 990 m   D) 999 m

    14. D

15. $\frac{1}{3}+\frac{1}{6}+\frac{1}{3}+\frac{1}{6}+\frac{1}{3}+\frac{1}{6} = (\frac{1}{3}+\frac{1}{3}+\frac{1}{3})+(\frac{1}{6}+\frac{1}{6}+\frac{1}{6}) = (1) + (\frac{1}{2}) = 1\frac{1}{2}$.
    A) $\frac{2}{9}$ B) $1\frac{1}{2}$ C) $2\frac{1}{2}$ D) $3\frac{1}{2}$

    15. B

Go on to the next page ⟫ **7**

16. An acute angle has a positive measure less than 90°. A) 89° B) 90° C) 91° D) 100°	16. A
17. Do multiplications before additions: $1 \times 2 + 3 \times 4 = 2 + 12 = 14$. A) $1 \times 2 + 3 \times 4$ B) $1 + 2 \times 3 \times 4$ C) $1 \times 2 + 3 + 4$ D) $1 + 2 \times 3 + 4$	17. A
18. The sum of three *consecutive* integers is 21. The integers must be $6+7+8$ and the smallest of these is 6. A) 5 B) 6 C) 7 D) 8	18. B
19. Subtract 1 from numerator *and* denominator; then $\frac{6}{7} < \frac{7}{8}$. A) $\frac{9}{10}$ B) $\frac{8}{9}$ C) $\frac{6}{5}$ D) $\frac{6}{7}$	19. D
20. In triangle ABC, $m \angle A = 60°$. Triangle ABC will be equilateral whenever the two sides that form $\angle A$ have equal lengths. A) $AB = AC$ B) $AB = BA$ C) $m \angle B + m \angle C = 120°$ D) $m \angle A + m \angle B + m \angle C = 180°$	20. A
21. To make 47¢ with the fewest number of coins, use 1 quarter, 2 dimes, and 2 pennies—for a total of 5 coins. A) 4 B) 5 C) 6 D) 7	21. B
22. If 150% of a certain number is 300, then $(2/3)(150\%) = 100\%$ of the number is $(2/3)(300) = 200$. A) 100 B) 150 C) 160 D) 200	22. D
23. The reciprocal of 2 is ½; the reciprocal of ½ is 2. The answer is D. A) less than 1 B) more than 1 C) odd D) positive	23. D
24. If *twice* the perimeter of a square is 28, then the perimeter of the square is 14 and a side is $14 \div 4 = 3.5$. A) 1.75 B) 3.5 C) 7 D) 14	24. B
25. $9 \times 11 = 99 = 100 - 1 = 10^2 - 1$. A) $10^2 - 1$ B) 10^2 C) $10^2 + 1$ D) 11^2	25. A
26. If it takes 6 specks to make a spot, the number of specks it will take to make $5\frac{2}{3}$ spots is $5\frac{2}{3} \times 6 = \frac{17}{3} \times 6 = 17 \times 2 = 34$ specks. A) 30 B) 32 C) 34 D) 36	26. C
27. 50% of $\frac{1}{50}$ is $\frac{1}{2}$ of $\frac{1}{50} = \frac{1}{2} \times \frac{1}{50} = \frac{1}{100} = 1\%$. A) 0.04% B) 1% C) 10% D) 25%	27. B
28. $1 - 0.99 = 0.01$; $1.1 - 1 = 0.1$; $1.011 - 1 = 0.011$; $1.009 - 1 = 0.009$. A) 0.99 B) 1.1 C) 1.011 D) 1.009	28. D
29. The rocketship flies $36\,000 \div 60 = 600$ km in 1 minute, which is 10 km in 1 second and 120 km in 12 seconds. A) $\frac{1}{3}$ B) 2 C) 12 D) 120	29. C

Go on to the next page ▐▌▐▌➡ **7**

30. In rhombus $ABCD$, $AB = 10$, so $BC = 10$. In $\triangle ABC$, $AC < AB+AC$, so $AC < 20$, and $\triangle ABC$'s perimeter < 40. A similar result holds for $\triangle ABD$. A) 40 B) 35 C) 30 D) 25	30. A
31. Every whole number from 1 through 999 has a reciprocal between 1 and 0.001. The reciprocal of 1000 is *equal* to 0.001. A) none B) 10 C) 100 D) 999	31. D
32. Since $4+5 = 9$ and $2 \times 10 = 20$, $9 < 20$ and choice C is correct. A) $4 \times 5 < 2 \times 10$ B) $4 \times 5 > 2 \times 10$ C) $4+5 < 2 \times 10$ D) $4+5 > 2+10$	32. C
33. There are six such numbers that begin with a 4. In decreasing size order, they are 4321, 4312, 4231, 4213, 4132, and 4123. A) 3421 B) 3412 C) 4123 D) 4132	33. C
34. Start with \$100. A 200% increase makes the price \$300. A 50% increase turns \$100 into \$150—which must then be doubled. A) 50% B) 100% C) 150% D) 200%	34. B
35. The smallest that three of the numbers could be is 0, 1, and 2. Their sum is 3. The next two could *then* be 43 and 44. A) 19 B) 41 C) 43 D) 89	35. C
36. In a sequence that never ends, each number after the first is half the preceding number. The first nine numbers are 16, 8, 4, 2, 1, 0.5, 0.25, 0.125, and 0.0625. You can't get D! A) 0.5 B) 0.125 C) 0.0625 D) 0.005	36. D
37. For the year 1992, John will get a \$5 allowance on Jan. 1, a \$5 allowance on Jan. 6, and \$5 every 5 days thereafter. Thus, John gets \$5 on Dec. 31, *the 366th day*—and $(365 \div 5) \times \$5 + \$5 = \$370$. A) \$73 B) \$365 C) \$366 D) \$370	37. D
38. In 6 hours, my clock will have gone 6 hours back, but the time will have gone forwards 6 hours, and my clock will be correct. A) 3 B) 6 C) 12 D) 24	38. B
39. If the circumference of a circle is numerically equal to the area of the same circle, $2\pi r = \pi r^2$. And, $2r = r^2$ if $r = 2$. A) 2π B) 2 C) 4π D) 4	39. B
40. $1 \times \dfrac{2}{3 \times \frac{4}{5 \times 6}} = 1 \times \dfrac{2}{3 \times \frac{4}{30}} = 1 \times \dfrac{2}{\frac{4}{10}} = 1 \times \dfrac{20}{4} = 5$. A) 5 B) 1 C) 0.8 D) 0.2	40. A

The end of the contest 🖎 **7**

Information & Solutions

Tuesday, February 2, 1993

7

Contest Information

- **Solutions** Turn the page for detailed contest solutions (written in the question boxes) and letter answers (written in the *Answers* column to the right of each question).

- **Scores** Please remember that *this is a contest, not a test*—and there is no "passing" or "failing" score. Few students score as high as 30 points (75% correct). Students with half that, 15 points, *deserve commendation!*

- **Answers & Rating Scale** Turn to page 123 for the letter answers to each question and the rating scale for this contest.

Copyright © 1993 by Mathematics Leagues Inc.

1. $1\,000\,000 - 1000 = 999\,000$.
   A) $99\,900$ B) $990\,000$ C) $999\,000$ D) $9\,990\,000$

   1. C

2. It rained all day every other day one week and it did not rain on the other days, so it could have rained on 3 or 4 days, 3/7 or 4/7 of the week.
   A) $\frac{1}{2}$ B) $\frac{2}{7}$ C) $\frac{4}{7}$ D) $\frac{6}{7}$

   2. C

3. $1234 - 345 = 889$.
   A) 889 B) 989 C) 999 D) 1111

   3. A

4. The year's 365th day is in Dec. Go back 65 days: it will be Oct.
   A) August   B) September   C) October   D) November

   4. C

5. $45\,455 \times 11 = 45\,455 \times (10+1) = 454\,550 + 45\,455 = 500\,005$.
   A) $50\,005$ B) $499\,905$ C) $499\,995$ D) $500\,005$

   5. D

6. When the cost of a candy bar increased from 25¢ to 29¢, the cost increase was 4¢, an increase of 4/25 or 16/100 or 16%.
   A) 4% B) 16% C) 20% D) 25%

   6. B

7. $12^2 + 43^2 = 144 + 1849 = 1993$.
   A) 1993 B) 1983 C) 110 D) 55^2

   7. A

8. The average of $\frac{8}{10}$ and $\frac{4}{10}$ is $\frac{6}{10}$, or $\frac{3}{5}$.
   A) $\frac{4}{15}$ B) $\frac{4}{7.5}$ C) $\frac{2}{7.5}$ D) $\frac{3}{5}$

   8. D

9. In a right triangle with legs of 8 and 15, the hypotenuse is 17, by the Pythagorean Theorem. The perimeter is $8+15+17 = 40$.
   A) 23 B) 40 C) 45 D) 46

   9. B

10. $\frac{2}{6} = \frac{8}{24}$, so $4 \times \frac{2}{6} = 4 \times \frac{8}{24} = \frac{32}{24}$.
    A) 8 B) 32 C) 48 D) 64

    10. B

11. If we subtract an acute angle from 90°, we get an acute angle.
    A) an acute   B) a right   C) an obtuse   D) a straight

    11. A

12. $99+98+97+96 = 100+100+100+100 - (1+2+3+4)$.
    A) $1+2+3+4$ B) $1+2+3$ C) $1+1+1+1$ D) 95

    12. A

13. To check divisibility by 4, you can check just the *last two* digits!
    A) $97\,531$ B) $55\,555$ C) $111\,111$ D) $54\,321$

    13. D

14. $\dfrac{1-\frac{1}{2}}{1+\frac{1}{2}} = \dfrac{\frac{1}{2}}{\frac{3}{2}} = \frac{1}{2} \div \frac{3}{2} = \frac{1}{2} \times \frac{2}{3} = \frac{1}{3}$.
    A) $\frac{1}{4}$ B) $\frac{1}{3}$ C) $\frac{1}{2}$ D) $\frac{2}{3}$

    14. B

15. The greatest common divisor divides *both* 2^5 and 2^6, so it's 2^5.
    A) 2^1 B) 2^5 C) 2^6 D) 2^{11}

    15. B

Go on to the next page ▐▶ 7

16. The sum of the three consecutive even integers 18, 20, and 22 is 60. The sum of the next three evens is $24 + 26 + 28 = 78$.

   A) 78   B) 72   C) 69   D) 66

   16.
   A

17. $\frac{1}{30} + \frac{29}{30} + \frac{7}{30} + \frac{23}{30} + \frac{11}{30} + \frac{19}{30} + \frac{13}{30} + \frac{17}{30} = 1 + 1 + 1 + 1 = 4$.

   A) 1   B) $3\frac{14}{15}$ C) $3\frac{29}{30}$ D) 4

   17.
   D

18. 10% of 90% is one-tenth of 90%, which is 9%.

   A) $\frac{9}{100}\%$ B) 9%   C) 100%   D) 900%

   18.
   B

19. Look at the choices, but remember the digits must be *different*.

   A) 999   B) 987   C) 978   D) 975

   19.
   B

20. $9^2 \times \sqrt{9} = 81 \times 3 = 243$.

   A) 27   B) 54   C) 81   D) 243

   20.
   D

21. All the numbers are equal, so the average is one of the numbers.

   A) 7   B) 11   C) 77   D) 84

   21.
   C

22. A square can be divided into 9 smaller congruent squares, as shown. By drawing different lines, it's possible to divide this square into 2^2 or 4^2 or 5^2 or $6^2 \ldots$ or 10^2 or $\ldots$ such smaller squares.

   A) 70   B) 80   C) 90   D) 100

   22.
   D

23. The ratio of 5¢ to 25¢ is 1:5, the same as 20¢ to 5×20¢.

   A) $1   B) $1.20   C) $1.25   D) $1.50

   23.
   A

24. The product is 1320. Since $10^3 = 1000$, the numbers are near 10. Since 1320 ends in 0, use 10 as one factor: $10 \times 11 \times 12 = 1320$.

   A) 10   B) 11   C) 12   D) 13

   24.
   C

25. Since $1+2+3+4+5+6+7+8 = 36$, the answer is $\sqrt{36}$.

   A) 9   B) $\sqrt{9}$ C) 36   D) $\sqrt{36}$

   25.
   D

26. I live on the planet Zork where, each second, every person flies the same distance as that person's height. If I can fly 100 meters in 20 seconds, my height is $100 \div 20 = 5$ meters.

   A) 1   B) 2   C) 5   D) 20

   26.
   C

27. In these 4 consecutive years, there is exactly one leap year, so $\#(1993) + \#(1994) + \#(1995) + \#(1996) = 3 \times 365 + 366 = 1461$.

   A) 1460   B) 1461   C) #(1997)   D) 7978

   27.
   B

28. Since $625 = 5^4$, 625 will divide evenly into $10^4 = 2^4 \times 5^4$.

   A) 10^3 B) 10^4 C) 10^5 D) 10^6

   28.
   B

29. To calculate $\frac{77}{777} \div 7$, divide the *numerator* by 7 to get $\frac{11}{777}$.

   A) 1   B) $\frac{11}{111}$ C) $\frac{77}{111}$ D) $\frac{11}{777}$

   29.
   D

Go on to the next page ‖➡ **7**

30. If the average of 4 positive numbers is 8, their sum is $4 \times 8 = 32$. If one were 2, the others would average 10—which is too large! A) 2 B) 3.5 C) 8 D) 9.9	30. A
31. *A, B*, and *C* are different non-zero digits. The sum is a 3-digit number, so $B \geq 5$. To get *B* as the sum's middle digit, use $B = 9$, $99 + 99 = 198$, and $C = 8$. $\begin{array}{r} BB \\ + BB \\ \hline ABC \end{array}$ A) 0 B) 6 C) 8 D) 9	31. C
32. Left side $= 2 \times 3 \times 2 \times 2 \times 5 \times 2 \times 3 \times 7 \times 2 \times 5 \times 2 \times 7$, so 2^6 is a factor. A) 2^3 B) 2^4 C) 2^6 D) 2^8	32. C
33. In a triangle, the longest side must be less than the *sum* of the other two sides, so the third side is 16, not 5. A) 21 B) 26 C) 37 D) 42	33. C
34. Two *different* whole numbers between 1 and 100 are multiplied together. Their product is *less than* $100 \times 100 = 10\,000$. A) 5 B) 4 C) 2 D) 1	34. A
35. The largest number will have the smallest denominator. A) $\frac{1}{\pi}$ B) $\frac{1}{2\pi}$ C) $\frac{1}{\pi^2}$ D) $\frac{1}{1993\pi}$	35. A
36. Since $10^{99} = 999\ldots999 + 1$, $10^{99} \div 9$ leaves a remainder of 1. A) 0 B) 1 C) 2 D) 3	36. B
37. Since $30 \times 30^2 = 30^3$, it takes $30^2 = 900$ 30's to equal 30^3. A) 30 B) 60 C) 90 D) 900	37. D
38. The perimeter of a square is equal to the circumference of a circle. If a diameter of the circle is 8, it's circumference is 8π, a side of the square is 2π, and the square's area is $(2\pi)^2 = 4\pi^2$. A) 16π B) $16\pi^2$ C) 4π D) $4\pi^2$	38. D
39. To simplify matters, let the Pros' season be 90 games. Of the first 30 games, they won 9. They must now win 36 of their final 60 games, and $36/60 = 60/100 = 60\%$. A) 60 B) 70 C) 75 D) 80	39. A
40. The pattern of the first 7 letters of *contestcontestcontest* . . . continues to the right. The 1992nd occurrence of a "*t*" is at the $(1992 \div 2) \times 7 = 996 \times 7 = 6972$nd letter of this pattern. The 1993rd occurrence of a "*t*" is at the $(6972+4)$th letter of the pattern. A) 6973rd B) 6974th C) 6975th D) 6976th	40. D

The end of the contest ✍ **7**

Information & Solutions

Tuesday, February 1, 1994

Contest Information

7

- **Solutions** Turn the page for detailed contest solutions (written in the question boxes) and letter answers (written in the *Answers* column to the right of each question).

- **Scores** Please remember that *this is a contest, not a test*—and there is no "passing" or "failing" score. Few students score as high as 30 points (75% correct). Students with half that, 15 points, *deserve commendation!*

- **Answers & Rating Scale** Turn to page 124 for the letter answers to each question and the rating scale for this contest.

Copyright © 1994 by Mathematics Leagues Inc.

1. $33\,333 + 77\,777 = 111\,110 = 55\,555 \times 2$.
   A) 1   B) 2   C) 5   D) 10

   1. B

2. Since $48 + 84 + 48 + 84$ is divisible by 4, and $1 + 1 + 1 + 1$ is also divisible by 4, the entire expression is divisible by 4.
   A) 0   B) 1   C) 2   D) 3

   2. A

3. $3^2 + 4^2 = 9 + 16 = 25 = 5^2$.
   A) 5^2 B) 7^2 C) 12^2 D) $2^2 + 5^2$

   3. A

4. To round 0.2345 to 3 places, change the 4 to a 5.
   A) 0.23   B) 0.24   C) 0.234   D) 0.235

   4. D

5. $1 + (10 \times 0) + (100 \times 0) + (1000 \times 0) = 1 + 0 + 0 + 0 = 1$
   A) 0   B) 1   C) 1111   D) 11 101

   5. B

6. Two whole numbers that are 4 apart and add up to 20 are 8 and 12. Their product is $8 \times 12 = 96$.
   A) 24   B) 60   C) 80   D) 96

   6. D

7. $2^3 + 2^2 + 2^1 = 8 + 4 + 2 = 14$.
   A) 12   B) 14   C) 2^6 D) 222

   7. B

8. The sum of *any* two sides exceeds the third side, so the third side must be *greater* than 5 (but not 7 or 12) and less than 19.
   A) 31   B) 26   C) 25   D) 23

   8. C

9. $999 + 9999 = (1000 - 1) + (10\,000 - 1) = 1000 + 10\,000 - (1 + 1)$.
   A) 1   B) 2   C) 1101   D) 111 + 1111

   9. B

10. There is a full moon once every 28 days. Since $13 \times 28 = 364$, we can have a 14th full moon on the 365th day.
    A) 12   B) 13   C) 14   D) 15

    10. C

11. $\frac{1}{2} \times \frac{1}{3} \times \frac{1}{6} = \frac{1}{6} \times \frac{1}{6} = \frac{1}{6} \div 6$
    A) 36   B) 6   C) 1   D) $\frac{1}{6}$

    11. D

12. There are equal numbers of nickels and quarters, and there are 7 such 30¢ groups in $2.10, so I have $7 \times 2 = 14$ coins.
    A) 7   B) 14   C) 21   D) 30

    12. B

13. All of the fractions have the value $0.333333 \ldots = \frac{1}{3}$, except A.
    A) $\frac{11}{30}$ B) $\frac{2}{6}$ C) $\frac{12}{36}$ D) $\frac{3}{9}$

    13. A

14. Since 4 of the 6 letters in the word "Arnold" are consonants, and $4 \div 6 = 0.666 \ldots \approx 0.67$, the answer is C.

    A) 33   B) 66
    C) 67   D) 70

    14. C

Go on to the next page ⫸ **7**

15. $3540 \div 60 = 59$, and 59 minutes before 3:58 P.M. is 2:59 P.M.
A) 1:59 P.M.   B) 2:57 P.M.   C) 2:59 P.M.   D) 4:57 P.M.

15. C

16. $(123 \times 999) - (122 \times 999) = (123 - 122) \times 999 = 1 \times 999 = 999.$
A) 122   B) 123   C) 999   D) 1000

16. C

17. Only $36 = 2^2 \times 3^2$ is a factor of $2^4 \times 3^2 = 144.$
A) 25   B) 27   C) 32   D) 36

17. D

18. $0.111 \times 1000 = 111; 0.11 \times 100 = 11; 0.1 \times 10 = 1;$ and $111 + 11 + 1 = 123.$
A) 321   B) 222   C) 123   D) 1230

18. C

19. Divide by 2 until you don't get an integer.
A) 16   B) 88   C) 444   D) 2222

19. A

20. 15 hundredths $= 15 \times 0.01 = 0.15$
A) 0.0015   B) 0.015   C) 0.15   D) 1500

20. C

21. Since $\frac{1}{2} + \frac{1}{3} = \frac{5}{6}$, its reciprocal is $\frac{6}{5} = 1.2$ (or, use a calculator).
A) 5   B) $\frac{5}{2}$ C) $\frac{5}{6}$ D) 1.2

21. D

22. Four monkeys are in a barrel. The sum of their ages 5 years ago was 80. The sum of their ages today is $80 + (5+5+5+5) = 100.$

A) 100   B) 89
C) 85   D) 84

22. A

23. Rewrite as $1 - \frac{1}{2} + \frac{1}{2} - \frac{1}{4} + \frac{1}{4} - \frac{1}{8} + \frac{1}{8} - \frac{1}{16} = 1 - \frac{1}{16} = \frac{15}{16}.$
A) 0   B) $\frac{1}{32}$ C) $\frac{1}{16}$ D) $\frac{15}{16}$

23. D

24. If the average of eight numbers is 10, their sum is 80. When we add 1, the 9 numbers total 81. Their average is $81/9 = 9.$
A) 9   B) 11   C) $\frac{81}{2}$ D) $\frac{11}{2}$

24. A

25. $\sqrt{16} + \sqrt{64} = 4 + 8 = 12 = \sqrt{144} = \sqrt{?}$, so $? = 144.$
A) 144   B) 80   C) 48   D) 12

25. A

26. Don't include the dotted line! The two sides of the triangle are 2 each. The *semicircle* has radius 1, so its circumference is $\pi r = \pi$. Add to get $4 + \pi.$
A) $2\pi + 4$ B) $\pi + 4$ C) $2\pi + 6$ D) $\pi + 6$

26. B

27. $1 + 2 + 4 + 8 + 16 + 32 + 64 = 127 = 128 - 1.$
A) 0   B) 1   C) 2   D) 3

27. B

28. Since the prime numbers between 1 and 1994 include both 2 and 5, their product is divisible by 10, and the remainder is 0.
A) 0   B) 1   C) 2   D) 9

28. A

29. $\frac{1+2+3}{4+5+6} \times \frac{8+10+12}{3+2+1} = \frac{1+2+3}{3+2+1} \times \frac{8+10+12}{4+5+6} = 1 \times \frac{2 \times (4+5+6)}{(4+5+6)} = 2.$
A) 8   B) 6   C) 2   D) $\frac{36}{21}$

29. C

Go on to the next page ⫸ **7**

30. $0.1\% = 0.1 \times 0.01 = 0.001$. A) 10 B) 0.1 C) 0.01 D) 0.001	30. D
31. 5 horses weigh as much as $5 \times 15 = 75$ dogs, and $25 \times 3 = 75$ dogs weigh as much as $25 \times 8 = 200$ cats. A) 40 B) 120 C) 200 D) 600	31. C
32. $\sqrt{1 \times 9 \times 9 \times 4} = \sqrt{1} \times \sqrt{9} \times \sqrt{9} \times \sqrt{4} = 1 \times 3 \times 3 \times 2 = 18$. A) $\sqrt{23}$ B) 18 C) 44.65 D) 1332	32. B
33. The smallest whole number larger than 1000 whose digits are all different is 1023, so its ones' digit is a 3. A) 0 B) 1 C) 3 D) 4	33. C
34. $\frac{7}{3} - \frac{3}{7} = \frac{49}{21} - \frac{9}{21} = \frac{40}{21}$ (or, by calculator, the answer is *almost* 2). A) $\frac{40}{21}$ B) $\frac{21}{40}$ C) $\frac{49}{9}$ D) $\frac{9}{49}$	34. A
35. Every integer n can be written as the sum of 1 and the integer just below n. But, these are *not* both positive if $n = 1$. A) 0 B) 1 C) 2 D) 49	35. B
36. Perimeter $= 14$, so two adjacent sides sum to 7. Area is the product of the same two sides, so 6×1, 5×2, and 4×3 work. A) 6 B) 8 C) 10 D) 12	36. B
37. In 4 hours, the hour hand has moved four-twelfths (or one-third) of 360°, which is 120°. A) 1440° B) 120° C) 90° D) 48°	37. B
38. $51+52+\ldots+100 = 1+2+\ldots+50 + 50$ more 50's $= 1275 + 2500$. A) 1325 B) 2525 C) 3775 D) 63750	38. C
39. Since $1000^2 = 1$ million and $3000^2 = 9$ million, the perfect squares that we want are the integers 1001^2, 1002^2, $\ldots$, 2999^2. Altogether there are 1999 such perfect squares. A) 1999 B) 2000 C) 2001 D) 3000	39. A
40. A 3-digit *upside down number* looks like one of the following: 1 ? 1, 2 ? 2, 5 ? 5, 6 ? 9, 8 ? 8, or 9 ? 6. For each of these 6 situations, there are 5 ways to fill in the ? part: use a 0, 1, 2, 5, or 8. The total number of ways is 6×5. A) 6×7 B) 6×5 C) $6 \times 5 \times 6$ D) $6 \times 7 \times 6$	40. B

The end of the contest 👉 **7**

Information & Solutions

Tuesday, February 7, 1995

7

Contest Information

- **Solutions** Turn the page for detailed contest solutions (written in the question boxes) and letter answers (written in the *Answers* column to the right of each question).

- **Scores** Please remember that *this is a contest, not a test*—and there is no "passing" or "failing" score. Few students score as high as 30 points (75% correct). Students with half that, 15 points, *deserve commendation!*

- **Answers & Rating Scale** Turn to page 125 for the letter answers to each question and the rating scale for this contest.

Copyright © 1995 by Mathematics Leagues Inc.

1. There are 4 groups of 1995+5 = $4 \times (1995 + 5) = 4 \times 2000 = 8000$. A) 1000 B) 2000 C) 4000 D) 8000	1. D
2. Since $1/5 = 0.20$, the value of $1/5$ is less than 0.25. A) $\frac{1}{5}$ B) $\frac{1}{4}$ C) $\frac{1}{3}$ D) $\frac{2}{7}$	2. A
3. The value of $5 \times \left(\frac{1}{3} + \frac{1}{3} + \frac{1}{3}\right)$ is $5 \times 1 = 5$. A) $\frac{5}{3}$ B) $\frac{5}{9}$ C) 5 D) $\frac{5}{27}$	3. C
4. The perimeter of the first figure is 10. Since every other figure has a perimeter of 12, figure A has the least perimeter. A) ⊞ B) ⊞ C) ⊞ D) ⊞	4. A
5. Do divisions before additions, so $2÷4 + 4÷8 = 1/2 + 1/2 = 1$. A) 2 B) 1 C) 0.5625 D) 0.03125	5. B
6. $120 = 5 \times 24$ and $336 = 14 \times 24$, so the gcd of 120 and 336 is 24. A) 6 B) 12 C) 24 D) 1680	6. C
7. By calculator, $11.111 + 1.11 + 0.1 = 12.321$. A) 11.322 B) 12.231 C) 12.321 D) 22.311	7. C
8. 543 min = 9 hrs 3 min after 3:45 PM = 12:48 AM A) 9:28 PM B) 12:48 AM C) 1:28 AM D) 1:48 AM	8. B
9. The sum of the whole number factors of 6 is $1+2+3+6 = 12$. A) 12 B) 11 C) 6 D) 5	9. A
10. $98765 + 12345 =$ 111110 (by calculator) A) 11110 B) 11111 C) 100000 D) 111110	10. D
11. Since 1 is *not* a prime, the sum *could* equal $2 + 3 = 5$. A) 2 B) 3 C) 4 D) 5	11. D
12. As shown, a small circle's diameter (with length 2) exactly overlaps a large circle's radius. The area of the shaded region = $\pi(2^2) - \pi(1^2) = 4\pi - \pi = 3\pi$. A) 2π B) 3π C) 5π D) 9π	12. B
13. $33 \times 333 = (11 \times 3) \times (111 \times 3) = 11 \times 111 \times 9$. A) 3 B) 6 C) 9 D) 27	13. C
14. $(13^2 - 12^2) - 3^2 = (169 - 144) - 9 = 25 - 9 = 16 = 4^2$. A) 2^2 B) 3^2 C) 4^2 D) 5^2	14. C
15. One-half of 50% of one-half equals $0.5 \times 0.5 \times 0.5 = 0.125$. A) 0.125 B) 0.25 C) 0.5 D) 12.5	15. A

Go on to the next page ▶ **7**

16. Since $\sqrt{91} = 9.539\ldots$, we know that $\sqrt{91}$ is not an integer. A) $\sqrt{0}$ B) $\sqrt{36}$ C) $\sqrt{49}$ D) $\sqrt{91}$	16. D
17. If equilateral triangle ABC has side $\overline{BC}$ in common with square $BCDE$, $m\angle ACD = 60° + 90° = 150°$. A) $270°$ B) $150°$ C) $140°$ D) $120°$	17. B
18. The choices differ from 8.01 by 0.01, 0.10, 0.11, and 1.00. A) 8 B) 8.1 C) 8.11 D) 9.01	18. A
19. Monday, cookies are 4 for \$1. Tuesday, they're 6 for \$1. For \$1, I get 2 more cookies on Tuesday. For \$6, I get 12 more. A) 2 B) 12 C) 24 D) 36	19. B
20. $32 \div 16 + 16 \div 8 + 8 \div 4 + 4 \div 2 = 2+2+2+2 = 8$. A) 2 B) 8 C) 16 D) 30	20. B
21. The length of a radius of a certain circle is 4. If A and B are two points on this circle, then AB could be any length ≤ 8. A) 1 B) 9 C) 10 D) 12	21. A
22. The sum is $8600 + 0.86 = 8600.86$. A) 86 860 B) 17 200 C) 8600.86 D) 860.086	22. C
23. $\dfrac{?}{95} = 1995 - \dfrac{19}{19} = 1995 - 1 = 1994$, so $? = 19 \times 1994 = 189\,430$. A) 1994 B) 1995 C) 189 430 D) 189 525	23. C
24. 50 pennies + 10 nickels + 5 dimes = 50¢ + 50¢ + 50¢ = \$1.50. A) 2 quarters B) 4 quarters C) 5 quarters D) 6 quarters	24. D
25. Pat the Cat runs at 5 m/sec and skates at 8 m/sec. Pat runs 80m in $80 \div 5 = 16$ secs. In that time, Pat can skate $16 \times 8 = 128$m. A) 50m B) 128m C) 240m D) 640m	25. B
26. Numerators and denominators all "cancel." A) 1 B) 3 C) 0.5 D) 0.25	26. A
27. Any number is always 100% of itself. A) 1 B) 39 C) 100 D) 3900	27. C
28. Cancelling, $1 \times 3 \times 5 \times 7 \times 9 = 945$. A) 1 B) 105 C) 315 D) 945	28. D
29. The students can sit in groups of 3, so it can't be choice D. With groups of 2 there's 1 left over, so it's not choice A. With groups of 5, there are 2 left over, so it's not choice B. The only choice left is choice C. A) 12 B) 21 C) 27 D) 29	29. C

30. The factors are 1, 2, 3, 4, 6, and 12. Their product is $12^3 = 1728$. A) 12 B) 36 C) 72 D) 1728	30. D
31. If $\frac{1}{4}$ of a number equals $\frac{1}{20}$, the number is $\frac{4}{20}$; and $\frac{5}{4} \times \frac{4}{20} = \frac{1}{4}$. A) $\frac{1}{4}$ B) $\frac{1}{5}$ C) $\frac{1}{16}$ D) $\frac{1}{64}$	31. A
32. 3700 days is slightly more than 10 years, and $1995 + 10 = 2005$. A) 2000 B) 2005 C) 2006 D) 2045	32. B
33. A cube with side–length 2 has volume $2^3 = 8$. A cube with side-length 4 has volume $4^3 = 64$; and 8 is 12.5% of 64. A) 0.125 B) 12.5 C) 25 D) 50	33. B
34. For any integer n, let $\blacklozenge n \blacklozenge$ be the sum of the squares of n's digits. Then, $\blacklozenge 345 \blacklozenge = 9+16+25 = 50 = 25+25 = \blacklozenge 55 \blacklozenge$. A) $\blacklozenge 12 \blacklozenge$ B) $\blacklozenge 55 \blacklozenge$ C) $\blacklozenge 60 \blacklozenge$ D) $\blacklozenge 444 \blacklozenge$	34. B
35. Every 2 seconds, a unicycle wheel of radius 1m rolls $2\pi(1) = 2\pi$ m. Thus, in 1 second, the wheel's average ground speed is π m/sec. A) 0.5π m/sec B) π m/sec C) 2π m/sec D) 4π m/sec	35. B
36. $\frac{1}{5 \times 2} + \frac{1}{5 \times 3} = \frac{1}{6}$, and $\quad 5 \times \frac{6}{5} = 6$, so A) 6 B) 1 the missing C) $\frac{5}{6}$ D) $\frac{6}{5}$ number is $\frac{6}{5}$.	36. D
37. A hexagon has 6 sides. An octagon has 8 sides. They'll both have perimeter 24 if their side-lengths are 4 and 3 respectively. A) 1:1 B) 2:1 C) 3:4 D) 4:3	37. D
38. The product cannot have a *repeated* prime factor, such as 2^2. A) $2^2 \times 11$ B) 5×11 C) $2 \times 3 \times 11$ D) 7×11	38. A
39. The least common multiple is $2^3 \times 3^2 \times 5 \times 7 = 2520$. A) 1 B) 1260 C) 2520 D) 3 628 800	39. C
40. There is 1 fraction with denominator 2, 2 with denominator 3, 3 with denominator 4, etc. On a calculator, $1+2+3+\ldots+44 = 990$. Now we begin to use denominator 46. The 10th such fraction with a denominator of 46 is 10/46. A) $\frac{8}{46}$ B) $\frac{9}{46}$ C) $\frac{10}{46}$ D) $\frac{11}{46}$	40. C

The end of the contest ✍ **7**

Information & Solutions

Tuesday, February 6, 1996

7

Contest Information

- **Solutions** Turn the page for detailed contest solutions (written in the question boxes) and letter answers (written in the *Answers* column to the right of each question).

- **Scores** Please remember that *this is a contest, not a test*—and there is no "passing" or "failing" score. Few students score as high as 30 points (75% correct). Students with half that, 15 points, *deserve commendation!*

- **Answers & Rating Scale** Turn to page 126 for the letter answers to each question and the rating scale for this contest.

Copyright © 1996 by Mathematics Leagues Inc.

1. $(1996 - 1996) \times (1996 + 1996) = 0 \times (1996 + 1996) = 0$. A) 0 B) 1996 C) 3992 D) 1996^2	1. A
2. Since 14 and 56 are multiples of 7, the multiple of 7 is 141 456. A) 141 427 B) 141 439 C) 141 441 D) 141 456	2. D
3. If Jan 1 falls on Sun, then Mar 1 will fall on Wed or Thur, and Mar 31 will fall on Fri or Sat, and March will have 5 Thursdays. A) 4 B) 5 C) 6 D) 7	3. B
4. A is the largest, as shown below. A) $500/100 = 5$ B) $40/10 = 4$ C) 3 D) $2000/1000 = 2$	4. A
5. $90 = 9 \times 10$ is the product of two consecutive whole numbers. A) 100 B) 99 C) 90 D) 80	5. C
6. The remainders are A) 6 B) 5 C) 4 D) 1. A) $776 \div 7$ B) $665 \div 6$ C) $554 \div 5$ D) $445 \div 4$	6. D
7. $(4 \times 888) - (4 \times 777) = (888 - 777) \times 4 = 111 \times \underline{4}$. A) 1 B) 4 C) 7 D) 8	7. B
8. We know that 24 pairs of pears is 48 pears. Since 6 bears ate equal numbers of these 48 pears, each bear ate $48 \div 6 = 8$ pears. A) 4 B) 6 C) 8 D) 16	8. C
9. There are 25% more new windows in my house than old ones. The ratio of new windows to old windows is $125\% : 100\% = 5 : 4$. A) 5:4 B) 9:4 C) 1:3 D) 25:1	9. A
10. $81 + 90 + 99 = 9 \times (9 + 10 + 11) = 9 \times 30$. A) 20 B) 30 C) 31 D) 32	10. B
11. $\frac{6}{5}$ of $6 = \frac{6}{5} \times \frac{6}{1} = \frac{36}{5}$. A) 5 B) $\frac{1}{6}$ C) $\frac{12}{5}$ D) $\frac{36}{5}$	11. D
12. Since $3456 \times 7 = 24\,192$, the hundreds' digit is a 1. A) 0 B) 1 C) 2 D) 4	12. B
13. A side of each square is 2 cm long. The perimeter of the figure contains 12 of these sides. A) 12 B) 24 C) 32 D) 40	13. B
14. $30 = 2 \times 3 \times 5$ has 3 *different* primes as factors, more than any other. A) 30 B) 32 C) 143 D) 144	14. A

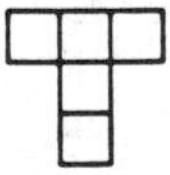

Go on to the next page ▐▐▊➡ **7**

15. Of the following sums, only the first is larger than 1000. A) 1995+0.1996 B) 199.5+1.996 C) 19.95+19.96 D) 1.995+199.6	15. A
16. $\sqrt{16 \times 25}$ = $\sqrt{16} \times \sqrt{25}$ = 4×5 = 20. A) $\sqrt{40}$ B) 10 C) 20 D) 100	16. C
17. Since 0.125 = 1/8, the numerator is 1. A) 1 B) 2 C) 5 D) 8	17. A
18. Since $(0.5)^2$ = 0.25, the number 0.5 is larger than its square. A) 0 B) 1 C) 2 D) 3	18. B
19. From 10:53 AM to 5:05 PM the same day is 6 hours 12 minutes. The time 3 hours 6 minutes after 10:53 AM is 1:59 PM. A) 1:54 PM B) 1:58 PM C) 1:59 PM D) 2:04 PM	19. C
20. 77 000 000 = $7 \times 11 \times 10^6$, so 11 is largest. A) 5 B) 7 C) 11 D) 77	20. C
21. My money doubles every day. I have $1 in my account today. It grows to $2, $4, $8, $16, $32, $64, $128, $256, then $512. The next day, the 10th day after today, it will first grow beyond $1000. A) 10 B) 999 C) 1000 D) 1024	21. A
22. Product = 123.????????, with 8 digits to the right of the decimal. A) 8 B) 10 C) 11 D) 12	22. C
23. Choices A and C are even, so they don't qualify. Only B leaves a remainder of 1 when divided by 2, by 3, by 5, or by 7. A) 2 + 3 + 5 + 7 + 1 B) $2 \times 3 \times 5 \times 7$ + 1 C) $2 \times 3 \times 5 \times 7 \times 1$ D) 23 571	23. B
24. If the winning number is $2^3 \times 3^2$, the winning number = 72 = 2×6^2. A) 2×6^2 B) 2×6^4 C) 6^5 D) 6^6	24. A
25. $\frac{1}{3} + \frac{10}{3} + \frac{100}{3} = \frac{111}{3}$ = 37. A) 10 B) 11 C) 33 D) 37	25. D
26. $10 \times 20 \times 30 = 1 \times 2 \times 3 \times 10^3$. A) 10 B) 30 C) 100 D) 1000	26. D
27. 10% of 100 = 10 = 1% of 1000. A) 1% B) 10% C) 100% D) 10 000%	27. A
28. Circumference + radius = $2\pi r + r = 6\pi + 3$ tells us that r = 3. The length of a diameter of this circle is 2×3 = 6. A) 3 B) 6 C) 2π D) $6/\pi$	28. B

Go on to the next page ⟫ **7**

83

29. The third angle is $180° - 130° = 50°$. The other two angles are $90°$ and $130° - 90° = 40°$. The smallest angle is $40°$.

   A) $20°$ B) $30°$ C) $40°$ D) $50°$

29.
  C

30. The circumference is 72π m, so diameter = 72 m and radius = 36 m. The triangular frame is 40 m high, so the ferris wheel's highest point is $40 \text{ m} + 36 \text{ m} = 76 \text{ m}$ off the ground.

   A) 56 m   B) 76 m   C) 112 m   D) 152 m

30.
  B

31. $\left(\frac{3}{2}\right) \times \left(\frac{4}{3}\right) \times \left(\frac{5}{4}\right) \times \left(\frac{6}{5}\right) \times \left(\frac{7}{6}\right) = \frac{7}{2} = 3\frac{1}{2}$.

   A) $\frac{1}{6}$ B) $\frac{1}{2}$ C) 2   D) $3\frac{1}{2}$

31.
  D

32. $68^2 = 4624$ and $62^2 = 3844$, so $68^2 - 62^2 = 780$.

   A) 30^2 & 40^2 B) 41^2 & 49^2 C) 62^2 & 68^2 D) 93^2 & 97^2

32.
  C

33. There are *two* factors of 3 in $666 = 2 \times 3^2 \times 37$.

   A) 666   B) 555   C) 222   D) 111

33.
  A

34. Mickey counted to 900 by 2's, beginning with 2. Minnie counted to 900 by 9's, beginning with 9. The numbers counted by both are those divisible by both 2 and 9. These total $900 \div 18 = 50$.

   A) 18   B) 50   C) 92   D) 100

34.
  B

35. If $12 = 2^2 \times 3$ is a factor of N^2, it's possible that $N^2 = 36$ and that $N = 6$. The number 4 is *not* a factor of 6.

   A) 2   B) 3   C) 4   D) 6

35.
  C

36. I have equal numbers of pennies, nickels, dimes, and quarters. I have at least 5 pennies, and 5 of each coin totals $2.05.

   A) 4   B) 5   C) 20   D) 41

36.
  C

37. $(1 \times 1 + \ldots + 1 \times 10) + (10 \times 1 + \ldots + 10 \times 10) + (100 \times 1 + \ldots + 100 \times 10)$
$= (1 + 10 + 100) \times (1 + \ldots + 10) = 111 \times (1 + 2 + \ldots + 10) = 111 \times 55$.

   A) 55   B) 60   C) 63   D) 66

37.
  A

38. 40 bears sing *and* dance; so 110 sing but don't dance, and 20 dance but don't sing, and $200 - 110 - 40 - 20 = 30$.

   A) 10   B) 20
   C) 30   D) 50

38.
  C

39. 1% of 1% = 1/100 of 1% = $(1/100)\%$.

   A) 1   B) 1%   C) $\frac{1}{100}$ D) $\frac{1}{100}\%$

39.
  D

40. $1 + 2 + \ldots + 999 + 1000 = (1 + 1000) + (2 + 999) + \ldots = 1001 \times 500 = 500\,500$.

   A) 0   B) 1   C) 4   D) 5

40.
  D

The end of the contest ☞ **7**

84

8th Grade Solutions

1991-92 through 1995-96

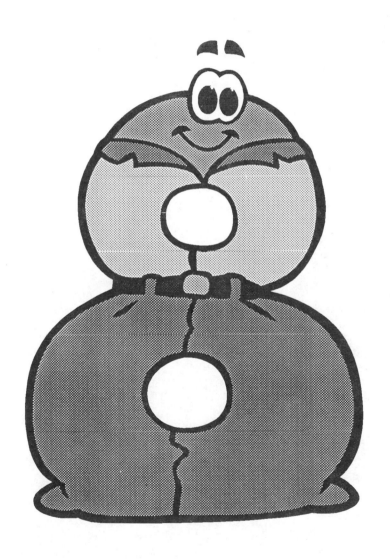

Information & Solutions

Tuesday, February 4, 1992

Contest Information

8

- **Solutions** Turn the page for detailed contest solutions (written in the question boxes) and letter answers (written in the *Answers* column to the right of each question).

- **Scores** Please remember that *this is a contest, not a test*—and there is no "passing" or "failing" score. Few students score as high as 30 points (75% correct). Students with half that, 15 points, *deserve commendation!*

- **Answers & Rating Scale** Turn to page 127 for the letter answers to each question and the rating scale for this contest.

Copyright © 1992 by Mathematics Leagues Inc.

1. $1000+100+10+1 = 1111 = 1100+11 = 11(100+1) = 11 \times 101$. A) 11 B) 100 C) 101 D) 111	1. C
2. The remainder is always the units' digit, which must be odd. A) 1 B) odd C) even D) prime	2. B
3. $1992 - 1000 = 992$, and $992 = 1000 - 8$. A) –1992 B) –8 C) 8 D) 1992	3. C
4. $111 \times 77 - 770 = 7777$, which *cannot* equal choice B. A) 101×77 B) 100×77 C) 707×11 D) 1111×7	4. B
5. $0.99 + 0.01 = 1$; so to make $0.99 + \underline{?} > 1$, $\underline{?}$ must be > 0.01. A) $\frac{1}{102}$ B) $\frac{1}{101}$ C) $\frac{1}{100}$ D) $\frac{1}{99}$	5. D
6. $50 \times 10 \times 0.1 \times 0.02 = (50 \times 0.02) \times (10 \times 0.1) = (1) \times (1) = 1$. A) 0.1 B) 0.2 C) 1 D) 10	6. C
7. Since $(\frac{1}{12}+\frac{1}{16}+\frac{1}{48}) = (\frac{4}{48}+\frac{3}{48}+\frac{1}{48}) = \frac{8}{48} = \frac{1}{6}$, its reciprocal is 6. A) $\frac{76}{3}$ B) $\frac{1}{76}$ C) 6 D) $\frac{1}{6}$	7. C
8. The average of the measures of the two *acute* angles in a right triangle is $\frac{1}{2}(90°) = 45°$. A) 30° B) 45° C) 60° D) 90°	8. B
9. $(-1 + 2) + (34 \times 56) + (78 + 9) = 1 + 1904 + 87 = 1992$. A) 1990 B) 1991 C) 1992 D) 1993	9. C
10. If the product of a certain number and 7 is 8, the *certain number* is 8/7. One-half of 8/7 is 4/7. A) $\frac{7}{16}$ B) $\frac{7}{4}$ C) $\frac{8}{7}$ D) $\frac{4}{7}$	10. D
11. $1000 \div 100 = 10$, and $10 = 100 \div 10$. A) 1000 B) 100 C) 10 D) 1	11. C
12. Jun. 1, 8, 15, 22, 29 are Fridays; Jun. 30 is Sat., and Jul. 1 is Sun. A) Sunday B) Saturday C) Friday D) Thursday	12. A
13. $0.222 + 0.333 + 0.444 = 0.999 = 1 - 0.001$. A) 0.999 B) 0.9 C) 0.1 D) 0.001	13. D
14. Midnight is 12 A.M., so 1 minute later is 12:01 A.M. A) 12:01 A.M. B) 12:01 P.M. C) 1 A.M. D) 1 P.M.	14. A
15. $(20 \times 40 \times 60) \div (2 \times 4 \times 6) = (20 \div 2) \times (40 \div 4) \times (60 \div 6) = 10 \times 10 \times 10 = 1000$. A) 1 B) 10 C) 100 D) 1000	15. D

Go on to the next page ⦀➡ **8**

16. The product of two negatives is positive, so the smallest is D. A) −100,−100 B) −50,−50 C) 75,75 D) 25,25	16. D
17. $\frac{1}{2} + \frac{1}{4} + \frac{1}{8} = \frac{4}{8} + \frac{2}{8} + \frac{1}{8} = \frac{7}{8}$, and $1 = \frac{7}{8} + \frac{1}{8}$. A) $\frac{1}{8}$ B) $\frac{1}{12}$ C) $\frac{1}{16}$ D) 0	17. A
18. Since the last factor, (10−10), is 0, the product equals 0. A) 10^5 B) $10^6−10^5$ C) 120 D) 0	18. D
19. 5¢ is 1/100 of $5, and 1/100 is 1%. A) 5 B) 1 C) 0.05 D) 0.01	19. B
20. 88 ÷ 5 = 17 3/5 = 17.6, which rounds to 18. A) 16 B) 17 C) 18 D) 20	20. C
21. Any integer divisible by 9 and 15 is divisible by 45. Since 45 is not even, it is not divisible by 6. So double 45 to get 90. A) 810 B) 90 C) 30 D) 15	21. B
22. 10% of 10 is 1, and $\frac{3}{2}$ of 1 is $\frac{3}{2}$, and $\frac{3}{2}$ = 1.5. A) 32 B) 15 C) 3.2 D) 1.5	22. D
23. 6÷5, 6−5 and 6+5 are not even integers; so the answer is not B, C, or D. Finally, an even integer times *any* integer is even. A) $M \times N$ B) $M \div N$ C) $M − N$ D) $M + N$	23. A
24. Since 20% means 1/5, 20% × 30% = (1/5)×30% = 6%. A) 6% B) 60% C) 600% D) 6000%	24. A
25. If ⅔ of the pail is filled, it will contain 6 liters of water. At the rate of ½ liter per minute, it will take 12 minutes. A) 2 B) 3 C) 6 D) 12	25. D
26. $9.9^2 − 9^2 − 0.9^2$ is approximately $10^2−9^2−1^2 = 100−81−1 = 18$. A) 18 B) 9 C) 8 D) 0	26. A
27. A line is drawn through the center P of rectangle $ABCD$, dividing it into two polygons. Since AB is not twice BC, the polygons *cannot* both be squares. A) squares B) rectangles C) trapezoids D) triangles	27. A
28. If we divide both fractions by 2, then $\frac{2}{3}:\frac{3}{4}$ becomes $\frac{1}{3}:\frac{3}{8}$. A) $\frac{3}{8}$ B) $\frac{1}{2}$ C) $\frac{8}{9}$ D) $\frac{3}{2}$	28. A
29. Since 1+2+3+4+5+6 = 21, the sum of 5 of these is not 21. A) 15 B) 18 C) 20 D) 21	29. D

Go on to the next page ⸺▶ **8**

89

30. The larger circle has a radius of 2, so its area is 4π. The smaller circle has a radius of 1, so its area is π. The difference, 3π, is the shaded region's area. A) 2π B) 3π C) 4π D) 7π	30. B
31. 1 day $= 60\times60\times24=86\,400$ sec, and $12\times86\,400$ is about 1 million. A) 1 day B) 12 days C) 1 month D) 12 months	31. B
32. If the 1st digit is 1, there are 6 ways: 1023, 1032, 1203, 1230, 1302, 1320. The 1st digit could also be 2 or 3, for a total of 18 ways. A) 12 B) 16 C) 18 D) 24	32. C
33. Consider $5\times7 + 1 = 36$. Since 36 is not odd, not prime, and not divisible by 8, the only possible answer is D. A) odd B) prime C) divisible by 8 D) divisible by 4	33. D
34. If the product of four consecutive integers is 0, then one of the integers must be 0; so the *smallest* such integer can't be 1. A) –3 B) –2 C) 0 D) 1	34. D
35. If the side of a *regular* (5-sided) pentagon is an integer, then the perimeter of the pentagon must be divisible by 5. A) 1992 B) 1993 C) 1994 D) 1995	35. D
36. Since 300 pages in 10 hours is 300 pages in 600 minutes, the rate is 1 page in 2 minutes or 5 pages in 10 minutes. A) 5 B) 10 C) 15 D) 30	36. A
37. If x is negative, for xy to be positive, y must be negative. A) $x < y$ B) $y > 0$ C) $y < 0$ D) $y > 1$	37. C
38. $1^{10}\times2^{10}\times5^{10} = 1\times2^{10}\times5^{10} = 2^{10}\times5^{10} = (2\times5)^{10} = 10^{10}$. Since 10^{10} is a 1 followed by 10 zeroes, 10^{10} is an 11–digit number. A) 10 B) 11 C) 20 D) 30	38. B
39. $0.05 = 1/20$. The primes < 20 (2, 3, 5, 7, 11, 13, 17, 19) have reciprocals > 0.05. (1 is *not* prime.) $1992-8 = 1984$ primes remain. A) 1972 B) 1984 C) 1985 D) 1988	39. B
40. If $\frac{1}{42} = a$, then $\frac{42}{30}\times\frac{1}{42} = \frac{42}{30}\times a$, or $\frac{1}{30} = \frac{7}{5}a$. A) $\frac{1}{12}a$ B) $\frac{7}{6}a$ C) $\frac{6}{7}a$ D) $\frac{7}{5}a$	40. D

The end of the contest ✍ **8**

Information & Solutions

Tuesday, February 2, 1993

Contest Information

8

- **Solutions** Turn the page for detailed contest solutions (written in the question boxes) and letter answers (written in the *Answers* column to the right of each question).

- **Scores** Please remember that *this is a contest, not a test*—and there is no "passing" or "failing" score. Few students score as high as 30 points (75% correct). Students with half that, 15 points, *deserve commendation!*

- **Answers & Rating Scale** Turn to page 128 for the letter answers to each question and the rating scale for this contest.

Copyright © 1993 by Mathematics Leagues Inc.

1. Counting decimal places, all have 4 places except choice D. A) 19.92×19.93 B) 1.992×199.3 C) 199.2×1.993 D) 1.992×1.993	1. D
2. $63 + 36 + 81 = 61+2 + 34+2 + 79+2 = 61+34+79 + 6$. A) 0 B) 2 C) 6 D) 12	2. C
3. All are larger than 1, except D, which equals 1. A) 7×0.7 B) 8×0.8 C) 9×0.9 D) 10×0.1	3. D
4. $2^1+2^2+2^3+2^4+2^5 = 2+4+8+16+32 = 62$. Now, add 2^1. A) 2^3 B) 2^2 C) 2^1 D) 2^0	4. C
5. $(10+20+30+40) \div (2+4+6+8) = 100 \div 20 = 5$ A) 2 B) 5 C) 10 D) 20	5. B
6. Since -6 is the smallest, its reciprocal, $-1/6$, is the largest. A) -6 B) -5 C) -4 D) -3	6. A
7. $\frac{3}{6} + \frac{3}{6} = 1 = \frac{3}{7} + \frac{4}{7}$. A) 3 B) 4 C) 6 D) 7	7. B
8. A triangle has *intersecting* sides, not parallel sides. A) triangle B) rectangle C) trapezoid D) square	8. A
9. $\frac{3}{8} \times \frac{5}{6} \times \frac{4}{5} = \frac{5 \times 3 \times 4}{5 \times 6 \times 8} = \frac{5}{5} \times \frac{3}{6} \times \frac{4}{8} = 1 \times \frac{1}{2} \times \frac{1}{2} = \frac{1}{4} = 0.25$. A) 0.2 B) 0.25 C) 0.5 D) 1	9. B
10. Remove the factors $2 \times 5 = 10$ from $2 \times 3 \times 4 \times 5 \times 6$ to divide by 10. A) $1 \times 2 \times 3 \times 4 \times 5$ B) $2 \times 3 \times 4$ C) $3 \times 4 \times 5$ D) $3 \times 4 \times 6$	10. D
11. If we subtract an acute angle from $180°$, we get an acute angle. A) an acute B) a right C) an obtuse D) a straight	11. A
12. 0.09×0.09 will have 4 decimal places. It will equal 0.0081. A) 8.1 B) 0.81 C) 0.081 D) 0.0081	12. D
13. Sam the Wonder Dog jumped on the table and ate $\frac{4}{5} = \frac{8}{10} = 80\%$ of my pie, so 20% remained. A) $\frac{1}{5}\%$ B) $\frac{4}{5}\%$ C) 20% D) 80%	13. C
14. $13^2 - 5^2 = 169 - 25 = 144 = 12^2$. A) 8^2 B) 10^2 C) 11^2 D) 12^2	14. D
15. The least number *divisible* by both 2^5 and 2^6 is 2^6. A) 2^5 B) 2^6 C) 2^{11} D) 2^{30}	15. B
16. $(-1)+101+(-2)+102+(-3)+103+(-4)+104+(-5) = 400-5 = 395$. A) 410 B) 400 C) 395 D) 390	16. C

Go on to the next page ➠ **8**

17. If 17% is 1.7, then 1% is 0.1 and 100% is $100 \times 0.1 = 10.0$. A) 1　　　B) 10　　　C) 17　　　D) 100	17. B
18. Since $2 = 2000/1000$, choice D is only $1/1000$ away from 2. A) $\frac{19}{10}$　　B) $\frac{21}{10}$　　C) $\frac{199}{100}$　　D) $\frac{1999}{1000}$	18. D
19. Each side is a whole number. In a square, $P = 4s$, so P is divisible by 4. To check divisibility by 4, just check the *last* 2 digits. A) 96　　　B) 152　　　C) 300　　　D) 462	19. D
20. If $2 \times 6 \times 30 \times 210 = 2 \times 2 \times 3 \times 2 \times 3 \times 5 \times 2 \times 3 \times 5 \times 7$ $= 2^4 \times 3^3 \times 5^2 \times 7^1$, so $a + b + c + d = 4 + 3 + 2 + 1 = 10$. A) 4　　　B) 9　　　C) 10　　　D) 12	20. C
21. The *addends* must have the ratio $\frac{1990}{1992} = \frac{950}{996}$, so choice D works. A) $\frac{1900+1}{1992+1}$　B) $\frac{1900+92}{1992+92}$　C) $\frac{1900+92}{1992+184}$　D) $\frac{1900+950}{1992+996}$	21. D
22. The average is 11, so their sum is $10 \times 11 = 110$. These same 10 numbers and 0 (now 11 numbers) average $110 \div 11 = 10$. A) 5　　　B) 5.5　　　C) 10　　　D) 11	22. C
23. 25% of 16% is the same as one-quarter of 16%, which is 4%. A) 4%　　　B) 9%　　　C) 41%　　　D) 400%	23. A
24. The sum of 5 even numbers is *always* even, so it's divisible by 2. A) 2　　　B) 3　　　C) 5　　　D) 10	24. A
25. Jane gets \$3.50 allowance weekly. She donates 1/7 of it (50¢) to charity and spends 1/7 of it (50¢) on lunches. Saving \$2.50 each week would require $210 \div 2.5 = 84$ weeks to save \$210. A) 60　　　B) 75　　　C) 84　　　D) 100	25. C
26. Since each of the nine small squares has a perimeter of 1, each has a side of 1/4. Each side of the larger square is $3 \times 1/4 = 3/4$. Finally, $4 \times (3/4) = 3$. A) 2.25　　　B) 3　　　C) 4.5　　　D) 9	26. B
27. $(88 + 1) \times (88 - 1)$ is $88^2 - 1$, a pattern which always holds. A) 87^2　　　B) 88^2　　　C) 89^2　　　D) $(88.5)^2$	27. B
28. A wheel has a circumference of 1 m. The wheel rolls 3 km = 3000 m without slipping, so it must roll a total of 3000 revolutions. A) 3　　　B) 30 C) 300　　　D) 3000	28. D
29. 9999 numbers are < 10 000. Eliminating 999 of them leaves 9000. A) 9000　　　B) 9990　　　C) 9999　　　D) 10 000	29. A

Go on to the next page ▐▐▌➡ **8**

30. *Any* 5 consecutive numbers must have factors 2 & 5, so ends in 0.
    A) 55 440   B) 55 444   C) 44 444   D) 45 454

30. A

31. Since $\pi/2 > 3/2$, $\pi/2 > 1$.
    A) $\dfrac{3}{\pi}$ B) $\dfrac{8}{\pi^2}$ C) $\dfrac{\pi}{2}$ D) $\dfrac{\pi}{\pi^2}$

31. C

32. Since 6 days ago was Wednesday, today is Tuesday. In 700 days, it will again be Tuesday. In 701 days, it will be Wednesday.
    A) Tuesday   B) Wednesday   C) Thursday   D) Friday

32. B

33. Since both angles at D are right angles, $\triangle ABD$ and $\triangle BCD$ are both right triangles. Using the Pythagorean Theorem, $AB = 20$ and $BC = 13$. The perimeter of $\triangle ABC$ is $5+16+20+13 = 54$.
    A) 33   B) 54   C) 56   D) 61

33. B

34. During both intervals from 11 to 1, the hands coincide once, at 12. During each of the other 20 hours, the hands coincide once.
    A) 2   B) 22   C) 23   D) 24

34. B

35. Since $365 \div 7$ is more than 52 (but less than 53), there must be *at least* 52 occurences of any day in each calendar year.
    A) 51   B) 52   C) 53   D) 54

35. B

36. There are 2 red, 3 blue, and 4 green marbles in a bag. I take one marble at a time out of the bag without looking. If I take 2 red, 2 blue, and 2 green marbles, then the very next marble must match one of the ones I already have, so I'll have 3 of one color.
    A) 3   B) 5   C) 7   D) 9

36. C

37. If a is 50% of b, $b = 2a$. If b is 25% of c, then $c = 4b = 4 \times 2a = 8a$.
    A) 75%   B) 100%   C) 150%   D) 800%

37. D

38. If $10+20+...+1000 = 50\,500$, $(10-1)+(20-1)+...+(1000-100) = 10+...+10\,000-(1+2+...+100) = 50\,500-(1/10)(50\,500) = 45\,450$.
    A) 40 400   B) 45 000   C) 45 450   D) 50 000

38. C

39. A *perfect cube* is an integer that can be expressed as the product of 3 equal integers. Of the first 1 million positive integers, the 100 integers $1^3, 2^3, 3^3, \ldots, 100^3$ (= 1 million) are *perfect cubes*.
    A) 100   B) 1000   C) 10 000   D) 333 333

39. A

40. In the four 30-day months, I got $4 \times \$(1+2+...+29+30) = 4 \times [(1+30)+(2+29)+...+(15+16)] = 4 \times \$(15 \times 31) = 4 \times \$465$. In the seven 31-day months, I got $7 \times \$(465+31)$. In Feb., I got $\$(465-30)$. Finally, $\$(4 \times 465 + 7 \times 496 + 435) = \$5767$.
    A) $5395   B) $5738   C) $5767   D) $5797

40. C

The end of the contest ✍ **8**

EIGHTH GRADE MATHEMATICS CONTEST

Math League Press, P.O. Box 720, Tenafly, New Jersey 07670-0720

Information & Solutions

Tuesday, February 1, 1994

Contest Information

8

- **Solutions** Turn the page for detailed contest solutions (written in the question boxes) and letter answers (written in the *Answers* column to the right of each question).

- **Scores** Please remember that *this is a contest, not a test*—and there is no "passing" or "failing" score. Few students score as high as 30 points (75% correct). Students with half that, 15 points, *deserve commendation!*

- **Answers & Rating Scale** Turn to page 129 for the letter answers to each question and the rating scale for this contest.

Copyright © 1994 by Mathematics Leagues Inc.

1. Each 1st group number is *twice* the corresponding 2nd group number.
   A) 2   B) 12   C) 63   D) 64

   1. A

2. 5 quarters + 5 pennies = $1.30 = 5 dimes + 16 nickels.
   A) 5   B) 10   C) 16   D) 80

   2. C

3. Using a calculator, 19.94 − 1.993 = 17.947.
   A) 0.01   B) 1.01   C) 17.947   D) 18.01

   3. C

4. The whole number divisors of 8 are 1, 2, 4, and 8. Their sum is 15.
   A) 16   B) 15   C) 8   D) 7

   4. B

5. In 7×284 = 1988 days, it's Tues. again. In 6 more days, it's Mon.
   A) Monday   B) Wednesday C) Thursday   D) Saturday

   5. A

6. 22÷2 = 11, which is larger than the other quotients.
   A) $\frac{1}{1}$ B) $\frac{22}{2}$ C) $\frac{444}{44}$ D) $\frac{8888}{888}$

   6. B

7. $\frac{1}{9}+\frac{1}{11} = \frac{11}{99}+\frac{9}{99} = \frac{20}{99}$, so its reciprocal is D (or use a calculator).
   A) 10   B) 20   C) $\frac{99}{2}$ D) $\frac{99}{20}$

   7. D

8. Since their sum is 0, the integers are opposites. Since their difference is 10, the integers are 5 and −5, and their product is −25.
   A) −25   B) 10   C) 5   D) 0

   8. A

9. Each angle is 60°. The sum of two of them is 120°.
   A) 180°   B) 120°   C) 90°   D) 60°

   9. B

10. Rewrite as $1 -\frac{1}{2}+\frac{1}{2} -\frac{1}{3}+\frac{1}{3} -\frac{1}{4}+\frac{1}{4} -\frac{1}{5} = 1 -\frac{1}{5} = \frac{4}{5}$.
    A) $\frac{1}{5}$ B) $\frac{1}{6}$ C) $\frac{4}{5}$ D) $\frac{5}{6}$

    10. C

11. $\sqrt{81} + \sqrt{100} + \sqrt{121} = 9+10+11 = 30 = \sqrt{900} = \sqrt{?}$, so ? = 900.
    A) 5.48   B) 17.38   C) 30   D) 900

    11. D

12. $10×0.1+100×0.09+1000×0.009+10\,000×0.0004 = 1+9+9+4 = 23.$
    A) 1.994   B) 2.3   C) 23   D) 1994

    12. C

13. Divide by 3 until you don't get an integer.
    A) 81   B) 999   C) 2727   D) 3333

    13. A

14. $(333×111) − (303×111) = (333−303)×111 = 30×111 = 10×333.$
    A) 30   B) 10   C) 3   D) 1

    14. B

15. 40% of 40 = 0.4 × 40 = 16.
    A) 1   B) 16   C) 40   D) 1600

    15. B

16. Since 125+250+375+500 is divisible by 5, and 1+1+1+1+1 is also divisible by 5, the entire expression is divisible by 5.
    A) 0   B) 1   C) 2   D) 4

    16. A

17. $\left(-\frac{5}{5}\right)×\left(-\frac{4}{4}\right)×\left(-\frac{3}{3}\right)×\left(-\frac{2}{2}\right) = (-1)(-1)(-1)(-1) = 1 = \frac{120}{120}.$
    A) 120   B) 1   C) −1   D) −120

    17. A

Go on to the next page ⭢ **8**

18.	Find the difference between each choice and 1.598. The least difference occurs with choice C. A) 1.589 m B) 1.590 m C) 1.600 m D) 2.000 m	18. C
19.	Lee multiplied a number by its square root. One way is to try each choice. Notice that $16 \times \sqrt{16} = 16 \times 4 = 64$. A) 4 B) 8 C) 16 D) 32	19. C
20.	The number $0.5 = 1/2$, and 50% of 1 is also $1/2$, so they're equal. A) 0.5% B) 25% C) 50% D) 100%	20. D
21.	A triangle has 3 sides, a pentagon has 5 sides, and a hexagon has 6 sides. All the others have 4 sides. A) #hexagon × #rhombus B) #pentagon × #triangle C) #square × #trapezoid D) #parallelogram × #rectangle	21. A
22.	Rewrite as $4 \times \frac{1}{4} \times 5 + 4 \times \frac{1}{5} \times 5 = 1 \times 5 + 4 \times 1 = 9$. A) 1 B) 2 C) 9 D) 18	22. C
23.	Robin computed the product $2 \times 2 \times 2 \times 2 \times 3 \times 4 \times 5 \times 5 \times 5 \times 5 \times 7$. This equals $(2 \times 5)(2 \times 5)(2 \times 5)(2 \times 5)(3 \times 4 \times 7) = 10\,000 \times 84 = 840\,000$. A) 8 B) 4 C) 2 D) 1	23. A
24.	The reciprocal of $-\frac{1}{2}$ is -2. The other reciprocals are larger. A) 1 B) $\frac{1}{2}$ C) -1 D) $-\frac{1}{2}$	24. D
25.	5 hours before 2:58 P.M. is 9:58 A.M. Now, give back 1 minute. A) 9:57 A.M. B) 9:59 A.M. C) 10:01 A.M. D) 10:57 A.M.	25. B
26.	The first 12 liters takes $12 \div 4 = 3$ minutes to make. The last 12 liters takes $12 \div 2 = 6$ minutes to make. Altogether, it takes $3 + 6 = 9$ minutes to make all 24 liters of soda. A) 4 B) 8 C) 9 D) 72	26. C
27.	30 is divisible by 2, 3, and 5; 36 is divisible by 2 and 3; 96 is divisible by 2 and 3; and 128 is divisible by 2 (only). A) 30 B) 36 C) 96 D) 128	27. A
28.	Choice D says that $2 < 1$. That is a false statement. A) $(-1) \times (-2) > (-1) + (-2)$ B) $(-1) \div (-2) < (-1) - (-2)$ C) $(-2) \div (-1) > (-1) + (-2)$ D) $(-1) \times (-2) < (-1) - (-2)$	28. D
29.	We must add together two radii and a quarter-circle. The sum of the two radii is $4 + 4 = 8$. The circumference of the *quarter*-circle is $2\pi r / 4 = 8\pi / 4 = 2\pi$. A) $8 + 2\pi$ B) $8 + 4\pi$ C) $16 + 2\pi$ D) $16 + 4\pi$	29. A

Go on to the next page ⇒ **8**

30. If the radius is π, the area is $\pi r^2 = \pi(\pi)^2 = \pi^3$. A) π B) 2π C) π^2 D) π^3	30. D

31. $\sqrt{16+\sqrt{81}} = \sqrt{16+9} = \sqrt{25} = 5$.

A) $\sqrt{97}$ B) 5   C) 13   D) $\sqrt{13}$

31. B

32. Since the areas of the squares are 9 and 16, the legs of the right triangle are 3 and 4, and the hypotenuse is 5.

A) 25   B) 7   C) 6   D) 5

32. D

33. $(3 \blacklozenge 4) = (3 \times 3) - 4 = 5$, and $(3 \blacklozenge 4) \blacklozenge 5 = 5 \blacklozenge 5 = (5 \times 5) - 5 = 20$.

A) 0   B) 6   C) 20   D) 35

33. C

34. The sum of an even number of odd numbers *must be even*, so the only possible sum of the 1994 odd numbers is choice B.

A) 1995   B) 1996   C) 2001   D) 2095

34. B

35. $\dfrac{88}{77 \times 66} = \dfrac{88 \div 100}{(77 \times 66) \div 100} = \dfrac{88 \div 100}{(77 \div 10) \times (66 \div 10)} = \dfrac{0.88}{7.7 \times 6.6}$.

A) $\dfrac{0.88}{7.7 \times 6.6}$ B) $\dfrac{0.88}{0.77 \times 0.66}$ C) $\dfrac{8.8}{7.7 \times 6.6}$ D) $\dfrac{8.8}{0.77 \times 0.66}$

35. A

36. The dimensions could be 1×2, 2×4, 3×6, etc. Checking, 6×12 gives a perimeter of 36. (The perimeter is always divisible by 6.)

A) 26   B) 27   C) 36   D) 44

36. C

37. Rewrite as $3989-1994 + 3988-1993 + \ldots + 1997-2 + 1996-1$ $= 1995 + 1995 + \ldots + 1995$, for a total of 1994 of the 1995's.

A) 1994×1994   B) 1994×1995   C) 1995×1995   D) 1994+1995

37. B

38. The product is even. Since the product is not divisible by 4, it must leave a remainder of 2 when divided by 4.

A) 3   B) 2   C) 1   D) 0

38. B

39. If $a \times a = 9$, then a could be –3, and $a \times a \times a$ would equal –27.

A) 18   B) 81   C) 729   D) –27

39. D

40. At the Belltower School, 99% of the 100 students are girls, so there are 99 girls and 1 boy. Since grade 8 is not all girls, the boy is in grade 8. If there are 49 girls and 1 boy in grade 8, 98% of the grade 8 students will be girls.

A) 98   B) 97

C) 49   D) 48

40. C

The end of the contest ✍ **8**

Information & Solutions

Tuesday, February 7, 1995

Contest Information

8

- **Solutions** Turn the page for detailed contest solutions (written in the question boxes) and letter answers (written in the *Answers* column to the right of each question).

- **Scores** Please remember that *this is a contest, not a test*—and there is no "passing" or "failing" score. Few students score as high as 30 points (75% correct). Students with half that, 15 points, *deserve commendation!*

- **Answers & Rating Scale** Turn to page 130 for the letter answers to each question and the rating scale for this contest.

Copyright © 1995 by Mathematics Leagues Inc.

1. $11111 = 10101 + \underline{\ ?\ }$ means that $\underline{\ ?\ } = 11111 - 10101 = 1010$.
   A) 101   B) 110   C) 1010   D) 110

   1. C

2. Numbers and their reciprocals always have the same sign.
   A) negative   B) positive   C) prime   D) 1

   2. A

3. $3 \times \left(\frac{1}{5} + \frac{1}{5} + \frac{1}{5} + \frac{1}{5} + \frac{1}{5}\right) = 3 \times 1 = 3$.
   A) 0.6   B) 0.12   C) 3   D) 15

   3. C

4. The area is a perfect square; so it cannot be a prime.
   A) even   B) odd   C) prime   D) 1

   4. C

5. $(1995 - 1994) \times (1994 - 1995) = 1 \times (-1) = -1$.
   A) –1   B) 1   C) –3990   D) 3990

   5. A

6. $(1000 \times 0.01) + (100 \times 0.001) + (10 \times 0.0001) = 10 + 0.1 + 0.001$.
   A) 1.0101   B) 10.101   C) 11.1   D) 1.11

   6. B

7. 1000 days is nearly 2¾ years = 2 years, 9 months. **Feb**
   A) October   B) November   C) December   D) January

   7. B

8. One-half of 1 thousandth = $\frac{1}{2} \times 0.0010 = 0.0005$.
   A) 0.5   B) 0.05   C) 0.005   D) 0.0005

   8. D

9. Convert each to a decimal; or note that $17/64 - 16/64 = 1/64$.
   A) $\frac{3}{8}$ B) $\frac{5}{16}$ C) $\frac{9}{32}$ D) $\frac{17}{64}$

   9. D

10. $\dfrac{1}{\frac{1}{2} + \frac{1}{3}} =$ $1/2 + 1/3 = 5/6$. Take the reciprocal to get 6/5.
    A) $\frac{6}{5}$ B) $\frac{5}{6}$ C) 6   D) 5

    10. A

11. If 20° is the vertex angle, the others are each 80°. If 20° is a base angle, the vertex angle is 140°. Choice B is not a possible angle.
    A) 20°   B) 40°   C) 80°   D) 140°

    11. B

12. $(10 \div 2) + (20 \div 4) + (40 \div 8) = 5 + 5 + 5 = 15 = 60 \div 4$.
    A) 15   B) 12   C) 5   D) 4

    12. D

13. Bob has 12 books. Jane has half as many, so Jane has 6 books. This is 3 times as many as Sue has, so Sue has 2 books.
    A) 2   B) 6
    C) 8   D) 18

    13. A

14. $(2+9)^2 = 11^2 = 121 = 2^2 + 9^2 + \underline{\ ?\ } = 85 + \underline{\ ?\ }$, so $\underline{\ ?\ } = 36 = 6^2$.
    A) 0^2 B) 6^2 C) 7^2 D) 11^2

    14. B

15. $\dfrac{11 + 22}{22 + 44} = \dfrac{33}{66} = \dfrac{1}{2} = \dfrac{11}{22} + 0$.
    A) 0   B) $\frac{22}{44}$ C) $\frac{11}{44}$ D) 1

    15. A

Go on to the next page ⇒ **8**

16. If I first increase five by one hundredth, and next I subtract one thousandth, I'll get 5 + 0.01 − 0.001 = 5.009.
    A) 4.999   B) 4.099   C) 5.099   D) 5.009

16.
D

17. Multiply first: 1+(1×1)+(1×2×1)+(1×1)+1 = 1+1+2+1+1 = 6.
    A) 6   B) 8   C) 16   D) 32

17.
A

18. If 40ℓ of maple sap are needed to make 1ℓ of maple syrup, then 1/40 = 0.025 = 2.5 percent of the sap is syrup.
    A) 0.025   B) 2.5   C) 25   D) 39

18.
B

19. 100×70×50 = 10×10×70×50 = (10×70)×(10×50) = 700×500.
    A) 7000×5000   B) 700×5000   C) 700×500   D) 7000×500

19.
C

20. Of 30 students, two-tenths got A's, so 0.2×30 = 6 got A's.
    A) 5   B) 6   C) 10   D) 20

20.
B

21. 25 pennies + 50 nickels + 100 dimes = $0.25 + $2.50 + $10.00 = $12.75 = 51 quarters.
    A) 7   B) 16
    C) 46   D) 51

21.
D

22. The least possible perimeter is 2+3+4 = 9. Notice that you *cannot* make a triangle whose sides are 1, 2, and 3.
    A) 3   B) 6   C) 9   D) 12

22.
C

23. 10% is 1/5 of 50%, and 1/5 = 20%, so 10% is 20% of 50%.
    A) 0.2   B) 5   C) 10   D) 20

23.
D

24. The product of a positive number and its reciprocal is always 1.
    A) prime   B) even   C) 0   D) 1

24.
D

25. The 1st area is ½(4)(1st base) = 2(1st base). The total is 2(1st base) + 2(2nd base) + 2(3rd base) + 2(4th base) = 2(AD) = 20.
    A) 5   B) 10   C) 20   D) 40

25.
C

26. If the average of 6 numbers is 7, these 6 have a sum of 42. If the average of all 7 numbers is 0, the 7th number is −42.
    A) −42   B) −7   C) −6   D) 0

26.
A

27. The product is positive and has 50 factors of 7 in the numerator.
    A) $50×7$ B) 7^2 C) $50×7^2$ D) $(-7)^{50}$

27.
D

28. Reducing, 88/888 = 11/111, which does not reduce.
    A) $\frac{1}{8}$ B) $\frac{1}{11}$
    C) $\frac{11}{111}$ D) $\frac{1}{800}$

28.
C

Go on to the next page ▐▐▐➡ **8**

29. There are 8 such factors. They are 1, 2, 3, 5, 6, 10, 15, and 30.
    A) 6   B) 7   C) 8   D) 9

29. C

30. $2^4 + 4^2 + 2^4 + 4^2 = 16 + 16 + 16 + 16 = 64 = 8^2$.
    A) 8^2 B) 8^{12} C) 12^{12} D) 12^{64}

30. A

31. $17\% = 17/100 = 5/100 \times 17/5 = 5\% \times 17/5$.
    A) $\frac{5}{17}$ B) $\frac{5}{17}\%$ C) $\frac{17}{5}$ D) $\frac{17}{5}\%$

31. C

32. 2 hr 59 min − 1 hr 31 min = 1 hr 28 min; and
    1:41 P.M. + 1 hr 28 min = 2:69 P.M. = 3:09 P.M.
    A) 3:09 P.M.   B) 3:19 P.M.
    C) 12:12 P.M.   D) 2:09 P.M.

32. A

33. Only 0 is its own additive inverse, so there's one such integer.
    A) none   B) one   C) two   D) three

33. B

34. The shaded region consists of (¾ of the circle) +
    (square − ¼ of the circle). This is $¾(4\pi)$ +
    $(4 − ¼ \times 4\pi) = 3\pi + 4 − \pi = 2\pi + 4$.
    A) $4\pi − 4$ B) $2\pi + 4$ C) $3\pi − 4$ D) π

34. B

35. Take products: $(0.5 \times 1) < xy \le (1 \times 2)$, or $0.5 < xy \le 2$, so $xy \ne 0.5$.
    A) 2   B) 1.5   C) 1   D) 0.5

35. D

36. Pattern: square roots of 18-digit integers have 9-digit integer parts.
    A) 999 999 999   B) 99 999 999   C) 9 999 999   D) 999 999

36. A

37. The average is the integer midway between 1 and 1995: it's 998.
    A) 997.5   B) 998   C) 998.5   D) 999

37. B

38. When running at J m/sec, John needs x/J secs
    to run x m. In the same time, at D m/sec,
    the dog can run $(D)(x/J) = Dx/J$ m.
    A) $\frac{Dx}{J}$ m   B) $\frac{Jx}{D}$ m

    C) $\frac{DJ}{x}$ m   D) $\frac{D}{xJ}$ m

38. A

39. Since $a^2 + b^2 = c^2$, $a^2 + b^2 + c^2 = c^2 + c^2 = 2c^2 = 800$, so
    $c^2 = 400$ and $c = 20$.

    A) $\sqrt{800}$ B) $\frac{1}{2}\sqrt{800}$ C) 25   D) 20

39. D

40. The lcm of the first 40 positive integers contains, as *additional* factors,
    only primes or powers of primes *not already* present in the first 30:
    31, 37, and the fifth 2 which is a factor of 32; and $2 \times 31 \times 37 = 2294$.
    A) 1147   B) 2294   C) 36 704   D) 89 466

40. B

The end of the contest ✍ **8**

EIGHTH GRADE MATHEMATICS CONTEST

Math League Press, P.O. Box 720, Tenafly, New Jersey 07670-0720

Information & Solutions

Tuesday, February 6, 1996

Contest Information

8

- **Solutions** Turn the page for detailed contest solutions (written in the question boxes) and letter answers (written in the *Answers* column to the right of each question).

- **Scores** Please remember that *this is a contest, not a test*—and there is no "passing" or "failing" score. Few students score as high as 30 points (75% correct). Students with half that, 15 points, *deserve commendation!*

- **Answers & Rating Scale** Turn to page 131 for the letter answers to each question and the rating scale for this contest.

Copyright © 1996 by Mathematics Leagues Inc.

1. $(10-9) \times (9-8) \times (8-7) \times \ldots \times (3-2) \times (2-1) = 1 \times \ldots \times 1 = 1.$ A) 1 $\qquad$ B) 9 $\qquad$ C) 10 $\qquad$ D) 11	1. A
2. Since both 12 and 24 are divisible by 12, 1224 is divisible by 12. A) 102 $\qquad$ B) 124 $\qquad$ C) 1122 $\qquad$ D) 1224	2. D
3. $0.5 + 0.05 + 0.005 = 0.555 = 555/1000 = 111/200.$ A) $\frac{111}{200}$ $\qquad$ B) $\frac{3}{200}$ $\qquad$ C) $\frac{111}{8}$ $\qquad$ D) $\frac{3}{8}$	3. A
4. April 1 was a Tues, so March 31, 24, 17, 10, and 3 were all Mondays. A) 3 $\qquad$ B) 4 $\qquad$ C) 5 $\qquad$ D) 6	4. C
5. A jogger who jogs exactly 100 steps per minute will take $450/100 = 4.5$ minutes to jog 450 steps. A) 4 $\qquad$ B) 4.5 $\qquad$ C) 5 $\qquad$ D) 5.5	5. B
6. Any non-zero number divided by itself equals 1. A) $\frac{1996}{6}$ $\qquad$ B) $\frac{1996}{9}$ $\qquad$ C) $\frac{1996}{12}$ $\qquad$ D) $\frac{1996}{1996}$	6. D
7. 9 hundredths $-$ 8 thousandths $= 0.090 - 0.008 = 0.082.$ A) 0.082 $\qquad$ B) 0.081 $\qquad$ C) 0.82 $\qquad$ D) 0.092	7. A
8. 367 days after February 28th is March 1 (leap year) or March 2. A) January $\qquad$ B) February $\qquad$ C) March $\qquad$ D) April	8. C
9. 0.0709, to the nearest thousandth, is 0.071. A) 0.0709 $\qquad$ B) 0.0701 $\qquad$ C) 0.070 $\qquad$ D) 0.071	9. D
10. $770 = 10 \times 77 = 2 \times 5 \times 7 \times 11,$ and $7 + 11 = 18.$ A) 14 $\qquad$ B) 16 $\qquad$ C) 18 $\qquad$ D) 21	10. C
11. Two-fifths of one-fifth of all wishes is $(2/5) \times (1/5) =$ $2/25 = 8/100 = \underline{8}\%$ of all wishes. A) $\frac{3}{5}$ $\quad$ B) $\frac{2}{25}$ $\quad$ C) 8 $\quad$ D) 60	11. C
12. $\frac{1}{3} + \frac{30}{9} + \frac{900}{27} = \frac{9+90+900}{27} = 37.$ A) 3 $\quad$ B) 37 $\quad$ C) 111 $\quad$ D) 999	12. B
13. If the equilateral triangles have sides of 2 cm and 3 cm respectively, the figure's perimeter is $3+3+2+2+1$ cm. A) 11 cm $\quad$ B) 12 cm $\quad$ C) 13 cm $\quad$ D) 15 cm	13. A
14. 100% of 10 = 10, and $10 = (10/1) \times (100)\% = 1000\%$ of 1. A) 1% $\qquad$ B) 10% $\qquad$ C) 100% $\qquad$ D) 1000%	14. D
15. $0.375 = 375/1000 = 3/8$ in lowest terms. Its numerator is 3. A) 1 $\qquad$ B) 3 $\qquad$ C) 5 $\qquad$ D) 8	15. B

Go on to the next page ⫸ **8**

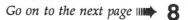

16. From 10:53 AM to 1:05 PM the next day is 26 hrs 12 mins, and 13 hrs 6 mins past 10:53 AM is B. A) 11:58 PM B) 11:59 PM C) 12:59 AM D) 1:59 AM 	16. B
17. The integers 1 and –1 are their own multiplicative inverses. A) 0 B) 1 C) 2 D) 3	17. C
18. Choice C differs from 1 by only 0.01. The others differ by more. A) 0.09 B) 1.011 C) $99 \div 100 = 0.99$ D) $100 \div 99 = 1.0101^+$	18. C
19. Negative numbers get smaller when they are doubled. A) negative B) even C) 0.5 D) a square	19. A
20. A 6 m by 3 m rectangle has area 18 m^2 and perimeter 18 m. A) 2 m B) 6 m C) 9 m D) 18 m	20. B
21. As shown below, only 81 has four factors of 3. A) $81 = 3^4$ B) $270 = 3^3 \times 10$ C) $999 = 3^3 \times 37$ D) $3333 = 3 \times 1111$	21. A
22. There are 2 uncool cats for every 3 cool cats. With 120 paws, there are $120/4 = 30$ cats altogether, of which 12 are uncool and 18 are cool. A) 12 B) 18 C) 30 D) 72 	22. B
23. There is a common factor of 3. A) 3^5 B) 15 C) 5 D) 3	23. D
24. $3^2 + 4^2 = 5^2$, so $3\,000\,000^2 + 4\,000\,000^2 = $ A. A) $5\,000\,000^2$ B) $7\,000\,000^2$ C) $12\,000\,000^2$ D) $25\,000\,000^2$	24. A
25. In a right triangle with area 12, each leg is as long as the side of a square. The triangle is half the square (draw the square's diagonal). A) 12 B) 24 C) 48 D) 144	25. B
26. When 7 is divided by 4, the remainder is 3. If 14 is divided by 4, the remainder is 2. This result is always true. A) 0 B) 1 C) 2 D) 3	26. C
27. The dimensions of a box are 3 by 4 by 5. Its volume is $3 \times 4 \times 5$. A) 60 B) 3600 C) $\sqrt{50}$ D) $\sqrt{60}$	27. A
28. Two pizzas cost as much as 3 cakes. One cake costs $6, so 3 cakes or 2 pizzas cost $18, and each pizza costs $9. A) $9 B) $30 C) $36 D) $45	28. D
29. Since $\frac{2}{3} + \frac{3}{2} = \frac{13}{6}$, its reciprocal is B. A) $\frac{13}{6}$ B) $\frac{6}{13}$ C) $\frac{6}{5}$ D) 1	29. B

Go on to the next page ⇒ **8**

30. One side = 6, one side > 6, and one side < 6. The sum of the two smallest sides < 12, so the perimeter < 24. [Possible triangle side-lengths are: A) 0.8, 6, 6.2; B) 5, 6, 7; C) 5.5, 6, 10.5.] A) 13 B) 18 C) 22 D) 24	30. D
31. $a \blacklozenge b = a + (2 \times b)$; $1 \blacklozenge (2 \blacklozenge 3) = 1 \blacklozenge [2 + (2 \times 3)] = 1 \blacklozenge 8 = 1 + 16 = 17$. A) 9 B) 11 C) 17 D) 36	31. C
32. The numbers counted by both are those divisible by both 6 and 4. Any number divisible by both 6 and 4 is divisible by 12. They both counted 12, 24, . . . , 600—a total of $600 \div 12 = 50$ numbers. A) 50 B) 100 C) 120 D) 250	32. A
33. Trial & error: 1 adult + 12 kids = \$27; 2 adults + 11 kids = \$28; 3 adult and 10 kid tickets cost \$29. A) 3 B) 5 C) 7 D) 10	33. D
34. $\frac{1}{4} = \sqrt{\frac{1}{16}} = \sqrt{\frac{4}{64}}$. A) 16 B) 4 C) 2 D) 1	34. B
35. The measure of the third angle that would make each isosceles: A) 70°, B) 45°, D) 60°. Choice C cannot become isosceles. A) 40° & 70° B) 45° & 90° C) 50° & 100° D) 60° & 60°	35. C
36. The two prime numbers between 110 and 130 are 113 and 127. A) 232 B) 240 C) 242 D) 246	36. B
37. If a 12-student class averaged 90 on a test, and a 20-student class averaged 80, all 32 students averaged $(12 \times 90 + 20 \times 80)/32$. A) 83.75 B) 84.75 C) 85.00 D) 85.75	37. A
38. $60 = 2^2 \times 3 \times 5$, so N^2 equals $2^2 \times 3^2 \times 5^2 \times$(possibly other factors). All primes in N^2 have even exponents. 16 need not be a factor. A) 16 B) 25 C) 36 D) 100	38. A
39. Sum = $1 \times (1 + \ldots + 10) + 2 \times (1 + \ldots + 10) + \ldots + 10 \times (1 + \ldots + 10)$. Factoring, this sum equals $(1 + \ldots + 10) \times (1 + \ldots + 10)$. Since $(1 + \ldots + 10) = 55$, the sum equals $55 \times 55 = 3025$. A) 2475 B) 2500 C) 3025 D) 3575	39. C
40. Add shaded regions: the lower left square + the one above it = 1 shaded square; the upper right square + the one below it = 1 shaded square; the 2 triangles + 2 fully shaded = 3 shaded squares. A) $3 + \pi$ B) $3 + \pi/2$ C) 6 D) 5	40. D

The end of the contest 8

106

Algebra Course 1 Solutions

1991-92 through 1995-96

Information & Solutions

Spring, 1994

Contest Information

- **Solutions** Turn the page for detailed contest solutions (written in the question boxes) and letter answers (written in the *Answers* column to the right of each question).

- **Scores** Please remember that *this is a contest, not a test*—and there is no "passing" or "failing" score. Few students score as high as 30 points (75% correct). Students with half that, 15 points, *deserve commendation!*

- **Answers & Rating Scale** Turn to page 132 for the letter answers to each question and the rating scale for this contest.

Copyright © 1994 by Mathematics Leagues Inc.

1. If $a = 1, l = 2, g = 3, e = 4, b = 5$, and $r = 6$, the value of $a + l + g + e + b + r + a$ is $1 + 2 + 3 + 4 + 5 + 6 + 1 = 22$.

   A) 7   B) 21   C) 22   D) 49

2. If $a = 0$, then C and D are 0, B is –1, and A is 1.

   A) $a + 1$ B) $10a - 1$ C) $1000a^2 + a$ D) $1000a^3 + a^2$

3. $(-1)^{100} = (-1)(-1)\times \ldots \times(-1)(-1) = 1$.

   A) –1   B) 1   C) –100   D) 100

4. $x+2+2x+4+3x+6+4x+8 = x+2x+3x+4x + 2+4+6+8 = 10x+20$.

   A) $x + 20$ B) $9x + 20$ C) $10x + 20$ D) $20x + 20$

5. $(y+2)(y-2) = y(y-2) + 2(y-2) = y^2 - 2y + 2y - 4 = y^2 - 4$.

   A) $y^2 - 4$ B) $y^2 - 2y + 4$ C) $y^2 + 2y + 4$ D) $y^2 + 4$

6. If $\frac{a}{b} = \frac{c}{d}$, then $\frac{a}{b} = \frac{c}{d} = \frac{a+c}{b+d}$. Thus, $\frac{1+2+3+ \ldots +100}{2+4+6+ \ldots +200} = \frac{1}{2}$.

   A) $\frac{1}{200}$ B) $\frac{1}{100}$ C) $\frac{1}{2}$ D) 100

7. If $y = 1994x + 1994$, then, when $y = 0$, $1994x + 1994 = 0$ and $x = -1$.

   A) –1   B) 1   C) –1994   D) 1994

8. $(x^2)(x^3)(x^4) = x^{2+3+4} = x^9$.

   A) x^5 B) x^9 C) x^{24} D) x^{234}

9. $x^2 - 10x + 24 = (x - 6)(x - 4)$

   A) $(x - 12)(x + 2)$ B) $(x - 6)(x - 4)$
   C) $(x + 12)(x - 2)$ D) $(x + 6)(x + 4)$

10. If $x = 10$, then $x^3+9x^2+9x+4 = 10^3+9(10^2)+9(10)+4 = 1994$.

    A) 23   B) 194   C) 204   D) 1994

11. $2\sqrt{3} = \sqrt{4}\sqrt{3} = \sqrt{12}$; $\sqrt{2}\sqrt{5} = \sqrt{10}$; and $\sqrt{3}\sqrt{3} = \sqrt{9}$.

    A) $2\sqrt{3}$ B) $(\sqrt{2})(\sqrt{5})$ C) $\sqrt{11}$ D) $(\sqrt{3})(\sqrt{3})$

Go on to the next page IIII➡ **A**

12. Note that $x = 1$ satisfies B and D, and $x = -1$ satisfies C. A) $x^2 + 1 = 0$ B) $x^2 - 1 = 0$ C) $x^3 + 1 = 0$ D) $x^3 - 1 = 0$	12. A
13. Since $x + 2y = 3$, we get $4x + 8y = 12$. Subtract $4x + 5y = 6$ to get $3y = 6$, or $y = 2$. A) –2 　　　 B) –1 　　　 C) 1 　　　 D) 2	13. D
14. The reciprocal of n is negative. The reciprocal of p is positive. A) $n > p$ 　 B) $-n > p$ 　 C) $\frac{1}{n} > \frac{1}{p}$ 　 D) $\frac{1}{n} < \frac{1}{p}$	14. D
15. I am thinking of a number. When I subtract 2 from the number, then take 300% of the result, the number I get is my original number. The equation is $3(x - 2) = x$, so $x = 3$. A) 0 　　　 B) 2 　　　 C) 3 　　　 D) 6	15. C
16. Since $n^2 + 2n + 1 = (n+1)^2$ and $n^2 - 2n + 1 = (n-1)^2$ and $9n^2 + 6n + 1 = (3n+1)^2$, the answer is C. A) $n^2 + 2n + 1$ B) $n^2 - 2n + 1$ C) $n^2 + 4$ 　　 D) $9n^2 + 6n + 1$	16. C
17. $\left(2 + \frac{1}{x}\right) \div \left(x + \frac{1}{2}\right) = \left(\frac{2x+1}{x}\right) \div \left(\frac{2x+1}{2}\right) = \frac{2}{x}$. A) $\frac{x}{2}$ 　　 B) $\frac{2}{x}$ 　　 C) $2x$ 　　 D) $\frac{1}{2x}$	17. B
18. $x^3 + x^2 + x + 1 = x^2(x + 1) + 1(x + 1) = (x^2 + 1)(x + 1)$. A) $x^2 + 1$ 　　　　　　 B) $x^3 - 1$ C) $x^3 + x^2 + x + 1$ 　　 D) $x^3 - x^2 + x - 1$	18. C
19. $x(x+1)+1 = x^2+x+1$. Twice more, multiply by x and add 1. A) $4x + 4$ 　　　　　　 B) $x^4 + 2x^3 + 3x^2 + 2x + 1$ C) $x^4 + 4$ 　　　　　　 D) $x^4 + x^3 + x^2 + x + 1$	19. D
20. Solve both $x+2 = 2x$ and $x+2 = -2x$. Don't forget to *check*! A) 0 　　　 B) 1 　　　 C) 2 　　　 D) 3	20. B
21. The solutions come from $(x - 2) = 0$, $(x - 1) = 0$, $(x + 1) = 0$, and $(x + 2) = 0$, so the solution set is $\{2,1,-1,-2\}$. A) 4 　　　 B) 5 　　　 C) 14 　　　 D) 120	21. A

Go on to the next page ⟾ **A**

22. $\sqrt{\sqrt{32}} = \sqrt{4\sqrt{2}} = 2\sqrt{\sqrt{2}}$.

    A) 2   B) $\sqrt{2}$ C) $2\sqrt{2}$ D) $2\sqrt{\sqrt{2}}$

    22.   D

23. There are 100 x's, and each *two* consecutive terms contribute –1.

    A) $100x - 1$ B) $100x - 25$ C) $100x - 50$ D) $100x - 100$

    23.   C

24. If $r = \dfrac{1}{d} = \dfrac{1}{2r}$, then $2r^2 = 1$, $r^2 = \dfrac{1}{2}$, and $\pi r^2 = \dfrac{1}{2}\pi$.

    A) $\dfrac{1}{2}\pi$ B) π C) 2π D) $\sqrt{2}\pi$

    24.   A

25. Since $(x+1)(x^2-x+1) = x^3+1$, it follows that $\dfrac{x^3+1}{x+1} = x^2-x+1$.

    A) x^2 B) $x^2 + 1$ C) $x^2 - 1$ D) $x^2 - x + 1$

    25.   D

26. $x^{32} - 1 = (x^{16} + 1)(x^{16} - 1) = (x^{16}+1)(x^8+1)(x^8-1)$. Continue.

    A) 1   B) $x + 1$ C) $x - 1$ D) $x^{16} + 1$

    26.   C

27. The surface area is $xy+xy + xy+xy + x^2+x^2 = 4xy+2x^2$. The volume is x^2y. The quotient, surface area divided by volume, is choice B.

    A) $\dfrac{2}{x} + \dfrac{4}{y}$ B) $\dfrac{4}{x} + \dfrac{2}{y}$ C) $\dfrac{2}{x+y}$ D) $x + 2y$

    27.   B

28. Since $(x-1)(x-2)(x-3)+(x-1)(x-2)(x-4)+(x-1)(x-2)(x+10) = (x-1)(x-2)[x-3+x-4+x+10] = (x-1)(x-2)(3x+3)$, 3 isn't a root.

    A) –1   B) 1   C) 2   D) 3

    28.   D

29. If 36 students took the exam, the average passing grade was 78, the average failing grade was 60, and the class average was 71, then $\dfrac{78(x) + 60(36 - x)}{36} = 71$.

    A) 14   B) 22   C) 24   D) 29

    29.   B

30. Plot points to graph $y = |x + 1| + |x - 1|$. The line $y = 2$ crosses this graph more than twice.

    A) 0   B) 1   C) 2   D) 3

    30.   C

The end of the contest ✍ **A**

Information & Solutions

Spring, 1995

Contest Information

- **Solutions** Turn the page for detailed contest solutions (written in the question boxes) and letter answers (written in the *Answers* column to the right of each question).

- **Scores** Please remember that *this is a contest, not a test*—and there is no "passing" or "failing" score. Few students score as high as 24 points (80% correct). Students with half that, 12 points, *deserve commendation!*

- **Answers & Rating Scale** Turn to page 133 for the letter answers to each question and the rating scale for this contest.

Copyright © 1995 by Mathematics Leagues Inc.

1. $10(10(10+9)+9)+5 = 10(10(19)+9)+5 = 10(199)+5 = 1995$.

   A) 995   B) 1005   C) 1995   D) 9950

   1. C

2. $(x+2)(x+2)(x-2)(x-2) = [(x+2)(x-2)]^2 = (x^2-4)^2$.

   A) $(x^2 - 4)^2$ B) $(x^2 + 4)^2$ C) $x^4 - 16$ D) $x^4 + 16$

   2. A

3. Since $(-1)^{odd} = -1$, the product $= (-1)(-1)(-1)(-1) = 1$.

   A) -24 B) -1 C) 1   D) 24

   3. C

4. By long division, it's $x^3 + 8$ (or, let $x = 1$).

   A) x^2+4 B) x^3+8 C) x^3-8 D) x^4+16

   4. B

5. Since the l.c.d. is 10^5, the answer is A.

   A) $\dfrac{11111}{10^5}$ B) $\dfrac{1}{10^6}$ C) $\dfrac{111111}{10^6}$ D) $\dfrac{1}{10^{15}}$

   5. A

6. $(x+3)(x-3)+(x+6)(x+3) = (x+3)[(x-3)+(x+6)] = (x+3)(2x+3)$.

   A) $x + 3$ B) $x + 6$ C) $2x + 3$ D) $2x + 6$

   6. C

7. Absolute value ≥ 0, so $|-x| = -2$ cannot have any solutions.

   A) none   B) 1   C) 2   D) 4

   7. A

8. When $2x + 4 = -4x - 2$, we get $x = -1$. When $x = -1$, $y = 2$.

   A) -1 B) 0   C) 1   D) 2

   8. D

9. Lee's rate is x m/sec, the dog's rate is $3x$ m/sec and Pat's rate is $3x+2$ m/sec. In 10 seconds, Pat runs $30x+20$ m and Lee runs $10x$ m, so Pat will be ahead of Lee by $20x+20$ m.

   A) $2x+2$ B) $20x+20$ C) $30x+20$ D) 20

   9. B

10. $x\%$ of $100\% = x\%$ of $1 = x\%$.

    A) x B) $x\%$ C) $10x$ D) $100x$

    10. B

11. Given $= x+5-x-4+x+3-x-2+x+1-x = 5-4+3-2+1 = 3$.

    A) -3 B) 3   C) $3x + 3$ D) $6x + 3$

    11. B

12. Since $(-1995)^2 = 1995^2 > 1995$, the largest is D.

    A) 1995   B) 1^{1995} C) $\left(\frac{1}{1995}\right)^2$ D) $(-1995)^2$

    12. D

Go on to the next page ➡ **A**

13. To equal 0 when $x = 2$ and when $x = 4$ requires factors of $(x-2)$ and $(x-4)$ in the numerator. Check A and B for $x = 7$.

A) $\dfrac{5(x-2)(x-4)}{(7-2)(7-4)}$

B) $\dfrac{7(x-2)(x-4)}{(5-2)(5-4)}$

C) $\dfrac{7(x-5)(x-5)}{(2-5)(4-5)}$

D) $\dfrac{4(x-5)(x-7)}{(2-5)(2-7)}$

13.

B

14.  $(x^1)^2(x^2)^3 =$ $x^2 x^6 = x^8$

A) x^8 B) x^{12} C) x^{15} D) x^{18}

14.

A

15. When $x = 50$, $(x - 1)(x - 2) \times \ldots \times (x - 98)(x - 99)$ has the value 0, since one its factors, $(x - 50)$, has the value 0.

A) $49!$ B) $(2)(49!)$ C) $(49!)^2$ D) 0

15.

D

16. Since the sum of two odd numbers is always even, no ordered pairs of positive odd integers (x,y) satisfy $x + y = 1995$.

A) none   B) 998   C) 1994   D) 1995

16.

A

17. The region in the xy-plane bounded by the graphs of $x = 1995$, $x = 1996$, $y = 1997$, and $y = 1998$ is a unit square of area 1.

A) 1   B) 1995   C) 1996   D) 1997

17.

A

18. $\dfrac{x+1+\dfrac{1}{x}}{x^2+1+\dfrac{1}{x^2}} = \dfrac{\dfrac{x^2+x+1}{x}}{\dfrac{x^4+x^2+1}{x^2}} = \dfrac{(x^2)(x^2+x+1)}{(x)(x^4+x^2+1)} = C.$

A) $\dfrac{1}{x}+1+x$ B) $1+\dfrac{2}{x}$ C) $\dfrac{x^3+x^2+x}{x^4+x^2+1}$ D) $\dfrac{x^2+x+1}{x^4+x^2+1}$

18.

C

19. When x is negative, inequality D is false.

A) $|x| + x \geq 0$ B) $-|x| \leq x$ C) $|x| - x \geq 0$ D) $|-x| \leq x$

19.

D

20. In the units' column, the sum N+N+E will have a units' digit of N if E = 9. In the tens' column, 1+U+O+H will have units' digit 7 if H = 4. Finally, in the hundreds' column, the sum 1+F+T = 1+2+3 = 6.

A) 4   B) 6   C) 8   D) 9

20.

B

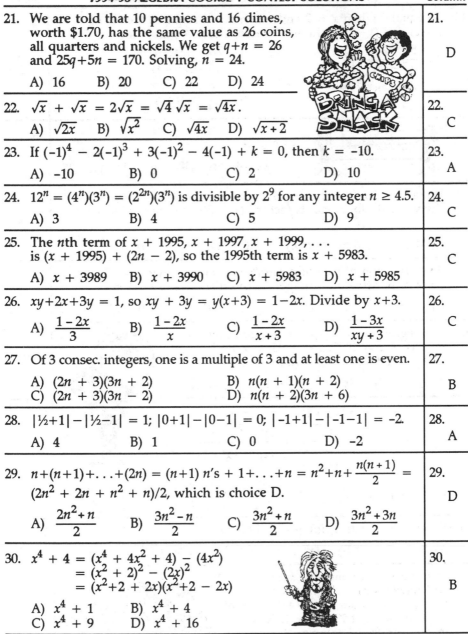

21. We are told that 10 pennies and 16 dimes, worth $1.70, has the same value as 26 coins, all quarters and nickels. We get $q+n = 26$ and $25q+5n = 170$. Solving, $n = 24$.

    A) 16   B) 20   C) 22   D) 24

    21. D

22. $\sqrt{x} + \sqrt{x} = 2\sqrt{x} = \sqrt{4}\sqrt{x} = \sqrt{4x}$.

    A) $\sqrt{2x}$ B) $\sqrt{x^2}$ C) $\sqrt{4x}$ D) $\sqrt{x+2}$

    22. C

23. If $(-1)^4 - 2(-1)^3 + 3(-1)^2 - 4(-1) + k = 0$, then $k = -10$.

    A) -10 B) 0   C) 2   D) 10

    23. A

24. $12^n = (4^n)(3^n) = (2^{2n})(3^n)$ is divisible by 2^9 for any integer $n \geq 4.5$.

    A) 3   B) 4   C) 5   D) 9

    24. C

25. The nth term of $x + 1995, x + 1997, x + 1999, \ldots$ is $(x + 1995) + (2n - 2)$, so the 1995th term is $x + 5983$.

    A) $x + 3989$ B) $x + 3990$ C) $x + 5983$ D) $x + 5985$

    25. C

26. $xy+2x+3y = 1$, so $xy + 3y = y(x+3) = 1-2x$. Divide by $x+3$.

    A) $\dfrac{1-2x}{3}$ B) $\dfrac{1-2x}{x}$ C) $\dfrac{1-2x}{x+3}$ D) $\dfrac{1-3x}{xy+3}$

    26. C

27. Of 3 consec. integers, one is a multiple of 3 and at least one is even.

    A) $(2n + 3)(3n + 2)$ B) $n(n + 1)(n + 2)$
    C) $(2n + 3)(3n - 2)$ D) $n(n + 2)(3n + 6)$

    27. B

28. $|\frac{1}{2}+1| - |\frac{1}{2}-1| = 1$; $|0+1| - |0-1| = 0$; $|-1+1| - |-1-1| = -2$.

    A) 4   B) 1   C) 0   D) -2

    28. A

29. $n+(n+1)+\ldots+(2n) = (n+1)$ n's $+ 1+\ldots+n = n^2+n+\dfrac{n(n + 1)}{2} = (2n^2 + 2n + n^2 + n)/2$, which is choice D.

    A) $\dfrac{2n^2+n}{2}$ B) $\dfrac{3n^2-n}{2}$ C) $\dfrac{3n^2+n}{2}$ D) $\dfrac{3n^2+3n}{2}$

    29. D

30. $x^4 + 4 = (x^4 + 4x^2 + 4) - (4x^2)$
    $= (x^2 + 2)^2 - (2x)^2$
    $= (x^2+2 + 2x)(x^2+2 - 2x)$

    A) $x^4 + 1$ B) $x^4 + 4$
    C) $x^4 + 9$ D) $x^4 + 16$

    30. B

The end of the contest **A**

Information & Solutions

Spring, 1996
Contest Information

- **Solutions** Turn the page for detailed contest solutions (written in the question boxes) and letter answers (written in the *Answers* column to the right of each question).

- **Scores** Please remember that *this is a contest, not a test*—and there is no "passing" or "failing" score. Few students score as high as 24 points (80% correct). Students with half that, 12 points, *deserve commendation!*

- **Answers & Rating Scale** Turn to page 134 for the letter answers to each question and the rating scale for this contest.

Copyright © 1996 by Mathematics Leagues Inc.

1. $M = 1, A = 9, T = 9, H = 6$, so $\sqrt{M+A+T+H} = \sqrt{25} = 5$.

   A) 5   B) 12.5   C) 25   D) 625

   1.
   A

2. $1 - \left(-(-(-2))\right) = 1 + 2 = 3$.

   A) –3   B) –1   C) 1   D) 3

   2.
   D

3. $x^2 = 1$, so $(x^2)^2+1 = 1^2+1 = 2$.

   A) 1   B) 2   C) 4   D) 5

   3.
   B

4. $\frac{x+2}{x+1} = 1 + \frac{?}{x+1} = \frac{x+1}{x+1} + \frac{1}{x+1}$.

   A) 1   B) x C) 2   D) $2x$

   4.
   A

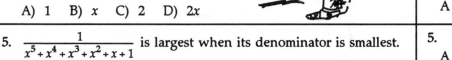

5. $\frac{1}{x^5+x^4+x^3+x^2+x+1}$ is largest when its denominator is smallest.

   A) 1996   B) 1997   C) 1998   D) 1999

   5.
   A

6. $\sqrt{(\sqrt{100})^2} = \sqrt{(10)^2} = 10$, so Terry sold 10 tee shirts.

   A) 10   B) 25   C) 50   D) 100

   6.
   A

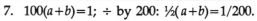

7. $100(a+b)=1$; ÷ by 200: $\frac{1}{2}(a+b)=1/200$.

   A) 0.5   B) 0.02   C) 0.002   D) 0.005

   7.
   D

8. Values are $-1+1+...-1 = -1$.

   A) 0   B) $(-1)^{100}$ C) $(-1)^{101}$ D) $(-1)^{4950}$

   8.
   C

9. $(100-1)(100-2)\times \ldots \times(100-100) = (100-1)\times \ldots \times(0) = 0$.

   A) 100!   B) 99!   C) 99   D) 0

   9.
   D

10. If my cat Boots has $5x$ upper teeth and $3y$ lower teeth, and if $5x = 3y$, divide by $5y$ to see that $x:y = 3:5$.

    A) 3:5   B) 5:3   C) 8:5   D) 3:8

    10.
    A

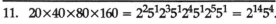

11. $20\times40\times80\times160 = 2^25^12^35^12^45^12^55^1 = 2^{14}5^4$.

    A) 17   B) 18   C) 19   D) 20

    11.
    B

12. The lcm of $(x-2)(x+2)$ and $(x-2)(x-2)$ is $(x-2)^2(x+2)$.

    A) $x - 2$ B) $(x - 2)(x + 2)$
    C) $(x - 2)^2(x + 2)$ D) $(x - 2)^3(x + 2)$

    12.
    C

Go on to the next page ⇒ **A**

13. If the product of the slopes of two perpendicular lines is *not* -1, then one line must be horizontal and the other must be vertical.

A) -1 B) 0 C) 1 D) 10

13.

B

14. $(x-1)^2 = 100\,000\,000\,000\,000$; so $x-1 = 10\,000\,000$, and $x = 10\,000\,001$.

A) $9\,999\,999$ B) $10\,000\,001$ C) $99\,999\,999$ D) $100\,000\,001$

14.

B

15. The number of different values of x which satisfy $(x^2 - 9)^3 = 0$ equals the number of different values of x which satisfy $x^2 = 9$. There are two values: $x = \pm 3$; so a box of cereal costs \$2.

A) \$6   B) \$3   C) \$2   D) \$1

15.

C

16. $\dfrac{1}{x-1} - \dfrac{1}{x+1} = \dfrac{x+1}{x^2-1} - \dfrac{x-1}{x^2-1} = \dfrac{2}{x^2-1}$.

A) 0 B) 1 C) 2 D) $2x$

16.

C

17. If (a,b) and (c,d) are the coordinates of different points on the graph of $3x + 4y = 5$, then $\dfrac{b-d}{a-c} =$ the slope of the line $= -\dfrac{3}{4}$.

A) $-\dfrac{3}{4}$ B) $\dfrac{3}{4}$ C) $-\dfrac{4}{3}$ D) $\dfrac{4}{3}$

17.

A

18. $\dfrac{2x^2+8x+8}{x^2+4x+4} = \dfrac{2(x^2+4x+4)}{x^2+4x+4} = \dfrac{2(x+2)^2}{(x+2)^2} = 2$ unless $x = -2$.

A) 0 B) 1 C) 2 D) more than 2

18.

B

19. The square root of x^{16} is x^8, so, unless $x = 0, 1$, or -1, choice C is not equal to the other choices.

A) $\sqrt{16x^{16}}$ B) $4\sqrt{x^{16}}$ C) $4x^4$ D) $4x^8$

19.

C

20. If $x + 3 = y$, then $x^2 + 6x + 9 = (x + 3)^2 = y^2$.

A) y^2 B) y^2-6x+9
C) y^2+6x+9 D) $y^2+12x+36$

20.

A

21. $10^{1996}-1 = 100\ldots00-1 = 999\ldots99$; and 1996 9's = choice C.

A) 1 B) $17\,955$ C) $17\,964$ D) $17\,973$

21.

C

22. When $x = 1, -1, 2$, or -2, the expression $\dfrac{2}{x}$ is an integer.

A) 1 B) 2 C) 3 D) 4

22.

D

Go on to the next page ⮕ **A**

23. If $r + \frac{1}{r} = s + \frac{1}{s} = 19 + \frac{1}{19}$, $r > s$, then $r = 19$, $s = \frac{1}{19}$, and $rs = 1$. | 23.

A) 0   B) 1   C) 19   D) 19^2

| 23. B |

24. $(x+y)^2 = x^2 + 2xy + y^2$. Squaring again,
$(x+y)^4 = (x^2 + 2xy + y^2)^2$
$= x^4 + 4x^3y + 6x^2y^2 + 4xy^3 + y^4$
Thus, the sum of the coefficients
of the five terms of $(x+y)^4$ is
$1 + 4 + 6 + 4 + 1 = 16$.

PECK!
PECK!
PECK!

A) 16   B) 12   C) 10   D) 9

| 24. A |

25. Squaring, $(2 + \sqrt{3})^2 = 7 + 4\sqrt{3}$.

A) $\sqrt{7} + \sqrt{1.18}$ B) $\sqrt{13.9282}$
C) 3.73205   D) $2 + \sqrt{3}$

| 25. D |

26. Since $s^2 = \pi r^2$, $s^2/r^2 = \pi$ and $s/r = \sqrt{\pi}$. Since diameter = $2r$,
divide both sides by 2 to get $s/2r = s/d = \sqrt{\pi}/2$.

A) $\sqrt{\pi}:1$ B) $2\sqrt{\pi}:1$ C) $\sqrt{\pi}:2$ D) $1:\sqrt{\pi}$

| 26. C |

27. $y = x+1$ intersects $y = |x|$ in just one point.

A) $y = x-2$ B) $y = x-1$ C) $y = x$ D) $y = x+1$

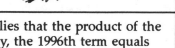

| 27. D |

28. $(x+y)^2 = 20^2$, so $x^2 + 2xy + y^2 = 400$.
Now subtract $x^2 + y^2 = 300$ to get
$2xy = 100$. Finally, divide both
sides by 2 to get $xy = 50$.

A) 15   B) 50   C) 75   D) 100

| 28. B |

29. $(x-a)(x-b) = x^2 - (a+b)x + ab = $
$x^2 - 5x + 3 = 0$, so $(a+b)(ab) = 5 \times 3$.

A) –20   B) 15   C) 20   D) 40

| 29. B |

30. The 1995th term is $\sqrt{1996}$. That implies that the product of the
first 1994 terms is also $\sqrt{1996}$. Finally, the 1996th term equals
(product of the first 1994 terms)(the 1995th term) = $\sqrt{1996}^2 = 1996$.

A $\sqrt{1995}$ B) $1996 \div 1995$ C) $1996 \div 2$ D) $\sqrt{1996}$

| 30. D |

The end of the contest ☞ **A**

Answer Keys & Difficulty Ratings

1991-92 through 1995-96

ANSWERS, 1991-92 7th Grade Contest

1. A	9. A	17. A	25. A	33. C
2. C	10. C	18. B	26. C	34. B
3. C	11. A	19. D	27. B	35. C
4. B	12. D	20. A	28. D	36. D
5. C	13. D	21. B	29. C	37. D
6. B	14. D	22. D	30. A	38. B
7. A	15. B	23. D	31. D	39. B
8. B	16. A	24. B	32. C	40. A

RATE YOURSELF!!!
for the 1991-92 7th GRADE CONTEST

Score	Rating
37-40	Another Einstein
34-36	Mathematical Wizard
31-33	School Champion
29-30	Grade Level Champion
26-28	Best In The Class
22-25	Excellent Student
18-21	Good Student
14-17	Average Student
0-13	Better Luck Next Time

ANSWERS, 1992-93 7th Grade Contest

1. C	9. B	17. D	25. D	33. C
2. C	10. B	18. B	26. C	34. A
3. A	11. A	19. B	27. B	35. A
4. C	12. A	20. D	28. B	36. B
5. D	13. D	21. C	29. D	37. D
6. B	14. B	22. D	30. A	38. D
7. A	15. B	23. A	31. C	39. A
8. D	16. A	24. C	32. C	40. D

RATE YOURSELF!!!
for the 1992-93 7th GRADE CONTEST

Score	Rating
36-40	Another Einstein
32-35	Mathematical Wizard
29-31	School Champion
26-28	Grade Level Champion
24-25	Best In The Class
20-23	Excellent Student
17-19	Good Student
14-16	Average Student
0-13	Better Luck Next Time

ANSWERS, 1993-94 7th Grade Contest

1. B	9. B	17. D	25. A	33. C
2. A	10. C	18. C	26. B	34. A
3. A	11. D	19. A	27. B	35. B
4. D	12. B	20. C	28. A	36. B
5. B	13. A	21. D	29. C	37. B
6. D	14. C	22. A	30. D	38. C
7. B	15. C	23. D	31. C	39. A
8. C	16. C	24. A	32. B	40. B

RATE YOURSELF!!!
for the 1993-94 7th GRADE CONTEST

Score	Rating
35-40	Another Einstein
31-34	Mathematical Wizard
28-30	School Champion
25-27	Grade Level Champion
22-24	Best In The Class
20-21	Excellent Student
17-19	Good Student
15-16	Average Student
0-14	Better Luck Next Time

ANSWERS, 1994-95 7th Grade Contest

1. D	9. A	17. B	25. B	33. B
2. A	10. D	18. A	26. A	34. B
3. C	11. D	19. B	27. C	35. B
4. A	12. B	20. B	28. D	36. D
5. B	13. C	21. A	29. C	37. D
6. C	14. C	22. C	30. D	38. A
7. C	15. A	23. C	31. A	39. C
8. B	16. D	24. D	32. B	40. C

RATE YOURSELF!!!
for the 1994-95 7th GRADE CONTEST

Score	Rating
37-40	Another Einstein
34-36	Mathematical Wizard
31-33	School Champion
27-30	Grade Level Champion
25-26	Best In The Class
21-24	Excellent Student
18-20	Good Student
15-17	Average Student
0-14	Better Luck Next Time

ANSWERS, 1995-96 7th Grade Contest

1. A	9. A	17. A	25. D	33. A
2. D	10. B	18. B	26. D	34. B
3. B	11. D	19. C	27. A	35. C
4. A	12. B	20. C	28. B	36. C
5. C	13. B	21. A	29. C	37. A
6. D	14. A	22. C	30. B	38. C
7. B	15. A	23. B	31. D	39. D
8. C	16. C	24. A	32. C	40. D

RATE YOURSELF!!!
for the 1995-96 7th GRADE CONTEST

Score	Rating
37-40	Another Einstein
34-36	Mathematical Wizard
31-33	School Champion
29-30	Grade Level Champion
25-28	Best In The Class
22-24	Excellent Student
19-21	Good Student
15-18	Average Student
0-14	Better Luck Next Time

ANSWERS, 1991-92 8th Grade Contest

1. C	9. C	17. A	25. D	33. D
2. B	10. D	18. D	26. A	34. D
3. C	11. C	19. B	27. A	35. D
4. B	12. A	20. C	28. A	36. A
5. D	13. D	21. B	29. D	37. C
6. C	14. A	22. D	30. B	38. B
7. C	15. D	23. A	31. B	39. B
8. B	16. D	24. A	32. C	40. D

RATE YOURSELF!!!
for the 1991-92 8th GRADE CONTEST

Score	Rating
38-40	Another Einstein
35-37	Mathematical Wizard
32-34	School Champion
28-31	Grade Level Champion
26-27	Best In The Class
22-25	Excellent Student
19-21	Good Student
15-18	Average Student
0-14	Better Luck Next Time

ANSWERS, 1992-93 8th Grade Contest

1. D	9. B	17. B	25. C	33. B
2. C	10. D	18. D	26. B	34. B
3. D	11. A	19. D	27. B	35. B
4. C	12. D	20. C	28. D	36. C
5. B	13. C	21. D	29. A	37. D
6. A	14. D	22. C	30. A	38. C
7. B	15. B	23. A	31. C	39. A
8. A	16. C	24. A	32. B	40. C

RATE YOURSELF!!!
for the 1992-93 8th GRADE CONTEST

Score	Rating
37-40	Another Einstein
34-36	Mathematical Wizard
32-33	School Champion
29-31	Grade Level Champion
27-28	Best In The Class
24-26	Excellent Student
20-23	Good Student
15-19	Average Student
0-14	Better Luck Next Time

ANSWERS, 1993-94 8th Grade Contest

1. A	9. B	17. A	25. B	33. C
2. C	10. C	18. C	26. C	34. B
3. C	11. D	19. C	27. A	35. A
4. B	12. C	20. D	28. D	36. C
5. A	13. A	21. A	29. A	37. B
6. B	14. B	22. C	30. D	38. B
7. D	15. B	23. A	31. B	39. D
8. A	16. A	24. D	32. D	40. C

RATE YOURSELF!!!
for the 1993-94 8th GRADE CONTEST

Score	Rating
38-40	Another Einstein
34-37	Mathematical Wizard
31-33	School Champion
28-30	Grade Level Champion
26-27	Best In The Class
23-25	Excellent Student
19-22	Good Student
15-18	Average Student
0-14	Better Luck Next Time

ANSWERS, 1994-95 8th Grade Contest

1. C	9. D	17. A	25. C	33. B
2. A	10. A	18. B	26. A	34. B
3. C	11. B	19. C	27. D	35. D
4. C	12. D	20. B	28. C	36. A
5. A	13. A	21. D	29. C	37. B
6. B	14. B	22. C	30. A	38. A
7. B	15. A	23. D	31. C	39. D
8. D	16. D	24. D	32. A	40. B

RATE YOURSELF!!!
for the 1994-95 8th GRADE CONTEST

Score		Rating
36-40		Another Einstein
33-35		Mathematical Wizard
30-32		School Champion
27-29		Grade Level Champion
24-26		Best In The Class
21-23		Excellent Student
18-20		Good Student
15-17		Average Student
0-14		Better Luck Next Time

ANSWERS, 1995-96 8th Grade Contest

1. A	9. D	17. C	25. B	33. D
2. D	10. C	18. C	26. C	34. B
3. A	11. C	19. A	27. A	35. C
4. C	12. B	20. B	28. D	36. B
5. B	13. A	21. A	29. B	37. A
6. D	14. D	22. B	30. D	38. A
7. A	15. B	23. D	31. C	39. C
8. C	16. B	24. A	32. A	40. D

RATE YOURSELF!!!
for the 1995-96 8th GRADE CONTEST

Score	Rating
37-40	Another Einstein
34-36	Mathematical Wizard
32-33	School Champion
29-31	Grade Level Champion
26-28	Best In The Class
23-25	Excellent Student
20-22	Good Student
15-19	Average Student
0-14	Better Luck Next Time

ANSWERS, 1993-94 Algebra Course 1 Contest

1. C	7. A	13. D	19. D	25. D
2. A	8. B	14. D	20. B	26. C
3. B	9. B	15. C	21. A	27. B
4. C	10. D	16. C	22. D	28. D
5. A	11. A	17. B	23. C	29. B
6. C	12. A	18. C	24. A	30. C

RATE YOURSELF!!!
for the 1993-94 ALGEBRA COURSE 1 CONTEST

Score	Rating
27-30	Another Einstein
24-26	Mathematical Wizard
21-23	School Champion
19-20	Grade Level Champion
17-18	Best In The Class
15-16	Excellent Student
12-14	Good Student
10-11	Average Student
0-9	Better Luck Next Time

ANSWERS, 1994-95 Algebra Course 1 Contest

1. C	7. A	13. B	19. D	25. C
2. A	8. D	14. A	20. B	26. C
3. C	9. B	15. D	21. D	27. B
4. B	10. B	16. A	22. C	28. A
5. A	11. B	17. A	23. A	29. D
6. C	12. D	18. C	24. C	30. B

RATE YOURSELF!!!
for the 1994-95 ALGEBRA COURSE 1 CONTEST

Score	Rating
27-30	Another Einstein
24-26	Mathematical Wizard
21-23	School Champion
19-20	Grade Level Champion
17-18	Best In The Class
15-16	Excellent Student
13-14	Good Student
10-12	Average Student
0-9	Better Luck Next Time

ANSWERS, 1995-96 Algebra Course 1 Contest

1. A	7. D	13. B	19. C	25. D
2. D	8. C	14. B	20. A	26. C
3. B	9. D	15. C	21. C	27. D
4. A	10. A	16. C	22. D	28. B
5. A	11. B	17. A	23. B	29. B
6. A	12. C	18. B	24. A	30. D

RATE YOURSELF!!!
for the 1995-96 ALGEBRA COURSE 1 CONTEST

Score	Rating
26-30	Another Einstein
23-25	Mathematical Wizard
20-22	School Champion
18-19	Grade Level Champion
16-17	Best In The Class
14-15	Excellent Student
11-13	Good Student
9-10	Average Student
0-8	Better Luck Next Time

Math League Contest Books
4th Grade Through High School Levels

Written by Steven R. Conrad and Daniel Flegler, recipients of President Reagan's 1985 Presidential Awards for Excellence in Mathematics Teaching, each book provides schools and students with:

- Easy-to-use format designed for a 30-minute period
- Problems ranging from straightforward to challenging
- Contests from 4th grade through high school

1-10 copies of any one book: $12.95 each ($16.95 Canadian)
11 or more copies of any one book: $9.95 each ($12.95 Canadian)

Use the form below (or a copy) to order your books

Name: _____

Address: _____

City: _____ State: _____ Zip: _____
                              (or Province) *(or Postal Code)*

Available Titles	# of Copies	Cost
Math Contests—Grades 4, 5, 6		
Volume 1: 1979-80 through 1985-86	_____	_____
Volume 2: 1986-87 through 1990-91	_____	_____
Volume 3: 1991-92 through 1995-96	_____	_____
Math Contests—Grades 7 & 8		
Volume 1: 1977-78 through 1981-82	_____	_____
Volume 2: 1982-83 through 1990-91	_____	_____
Math Contests—7, 8, & Algebra Course 1		
Volume 3: 1991-92 through 1995-96	_____	_____
Math Contests—High School		
Volume 1: 1977-78 through 1981-82	_____	_____
Volume 2: 1982-83 through 1990-91	_____	_____
Volume 3: 1991-92 through 1995-96	_____	_____
Shipping and Handling		$3.00

Please allow 4-6 weeks for delivery   Total: $_____

☐ Check or Purchase Order Enclosed; *or*

☐ Visa / MasterCard # _____

☐ Exp. Date_____ Signature _____

Mail your order with payment to:
Math League Press
P.O. Box 720
Tenafly, NJ USA 07670
Phone: (201) 568-6328 • Fax: (201) 816-0125